"Bill Bridges knows how firms can make [...] them. The first real publishing breakthrou[gh in] management in my thirty years of teaching how to prosper ... seeming chaos. A classic."
—**John Crystal**
Chairman, Crystal-Barkley Corporation
Coauthor of *Where Do I Go from Here with My Life*

"We live in a business era where changes in corporate strategies, structures, missions, and ownerships are accelerating at a bewildering rate. Bill Bridges succeeds in focusing our attention on the human factors that are vital in making transitions work."
—**Glenn Smythe**
Vice President
Fuchs, Cuthrell & Co., Inc.

"Government by its nature is in a constant state of transition and managing in that environment is filled with challenging paradoxes. Although Bridges emphasizes the corporate environment, its priceless insights into key issues that must be dealt with are invaluable for all managers."
—**Sandra J. Hale**
Commissioner of Administration
State of Minnesota

"*Surviving Corporate Transition* is a book for anyone involved in mergers or acquisitions who is interested in the successful integration and development of the business acquired. It can help both the individuals and the organization to survive and thrive in a corporate transition. Interesting, useful, and very readable."
—**Walter R. Trosin**
Vice President, Human Resources
Merck & Co., Inc.

Additional copies available through:
William Bridges & Associates
38 Miller Avenue, Suite 12
Mill Valley, CA   94941
(415) 381-9663

SURVIVING CORPORATE TRANSITION

WILLIAM BRIDGES, Ph.D.

"*Surviving Corporate Transition* takes a lot of the mystery out of transition management. Careful implementation of Dr. Bridges' suggestions should give any organization a significant strategic advantage over its competitors."

>—**Thomas E. O'Reilly**
>Vice President
>Director, Executive Resources
>The Chase Manhattan Bank, N.A.

"Bill Bridges' experience with companies in transition brings a sense of calm and purpose to a period of time that can otherwise be full of fear, conflict, and uncertainty. If you are experiencing change, this book is well worth your while."

>—**Robert H. Hood, Jr.**
>Vice President
>Aerospace Group
>Business Development
>McDonnell Douglas Corp.

"*Surviving Corporate Transition* provides a really pragmatic insight into understanding and managing the process of individual transition and organizational change."

>—**Don Martin**
>Vice President, Administration
>Ball Corporation
>Technical Products Group

"Bill Bridges' latest work is extraordinarily timely. *Surviving Corporate Transition* provides keen insights into the transition process and some very practical tools to help operating managers minimize the human and corporate costs associated with these difficult transitions."

>—**E. William Swanson**
>President
>SFA Management Corporation

"This book is about change and how to survive and/or adapt to it. It is must reading for executives who have to deal with change, and have been confounded, puzzled, and affected by it, and who would like to capitalize on it."

>—**Reyer A. Swaak**
>Vice President
>Human Resource Services
>Schering-Plough

SURVIVING CORPORATE TRANSITION

*Rational Management
in a World of Mergers,
Layoffs, Start-ups,
Takeovers, Divestitures,
Deregulation, and
New Technologies*

WILLIAM BRIDGES, Ph.D.

WILLIAM BRIDGES & ASSOCIATES

MILL VALLEY, CALIFORNIA

Published by William Bridges and Associates
Originally Published by Doubleday

Bridges, William, 1933-
Surviving corporate transition.

   Includes index.
   1. Industrial management.   2. Crisis management.
I. Title
HD31.B7395   1988   658.4'06   87-19978

CONTENTS

INTRODUCTION

My first real job was as an administrator at a small eastern college, and one of my duties there was to serve on the college's Academic Policy Committee. Being a twenty-five-year-old novice, I had a number of insights about the nature of teaching and learning which I was not unwilling to share with my new colleagues. At the first meeting of the APC, as it was called, I found myself in the middle of a hot debate about a proposal to cut the academic week from six days to five. (Back in the fifties, you may remember, Saturday morning classes were still regarded as part of the original Creation Plan on many campuses.)

It seemed to me that the case against them was embarrassingly obvious. First, the students hated them and skipped them regularly in spite of fairly severe penalties for too many cuts. Second, Saturday classes sliced into faculty weekends too. Third, keeping the classroom buildings warm and lighted on the weekends raised utility bills. Fourth (and not unrelated to third) the president of the college wanted us to end the Saturday classes. Finally (as I explained in fascinating detail) there really were some subjects that could be better taught in two longer classes per week than in three shorter classes. So why not have fifty-minute classes on Monday, Wednesday, and Friday and seventy-five-minute classes on Tuesday and Thursday?

My colleagues had a lot of trouble getting the point, I noticed. They remarked that we did not know the actual percentage of students who wanted to do away with Saturday classes. They commented that they themselves had attended Saturday classes at Harvard, Yale, and elsewhere. They remarked that the president's approach to academic issues was dangerously utilitarian. (Heat + Lights = Utilitarian . . . heh, heh, heh!)

Just as I was about to slip into a light coma, one of the professors said testily, "If we shifted to those two longer classes for half the subjects, I'd have to revise a lot of my lecture notes!" I still remember my amazement as I watched everyone nod, table the motion, and move on to a discussion of the Declining Literacy of Entering Students.

What was going on here? Were my elders self-serving impostors, purporting to care about their students and about higher education but really concerned with conserving the value of last year's notes? Or were they by nature so reactionary that they resisted any change as a matter of policy? Or were they stupid?

I think that this incident was the beginning of my fascination with organizational change—or, more precisely, with the way that organizational change does *not* happen, even though everything suggests that it ought to. My interest in these issues has grown into a career as a consultant specializing in the management of organizational transition.

Since those early days, I have learned a great deal more about why people do and do not change, what they do to keep from changing, and what they do to punish their organizations for forcing them to change when they do not want to. And I have learned that my former colleagues were not simply self-serving, reactionary, and stupid. They were doing the same thing that the president was doing in worrying about utility bills, the students were doing in fighting for their Saturdays, and I was doing in trying to show my elders that they were wrong. They were struggling to legitimate and protect their identity, their sense of meaning, their world.

I have also learned how self-defeating are our attempts to overcome the resistance to change are unless we recognize its world-protecting basis. The failure of our attempts may not be evident quickly, for we often do produce compliant behavior, or at least the appearance of it. But in the long run, we are likely to produce only more evidence for the old saw that the more things change, the more they stay the same.

We are particularly likely to underestimate people's ability to resist change when the need for it is so obvious that it is hard to imagine any logical arguments against it. But logic is often beside the point, as one can see from the case of the Colt .45.*

The .45 is the pistol that the U.S. Army used from 1911 until early 1985. By any objective standard, it was an out-of-date, heavy, unsafe, inaccurate handgun. It had originally been chosen because it was powerful enough to drop a horse in its tracks. (World War I hadn't yet put an end to the mounted cavalry in 1911.) In an age of constant innovation in weaponry, the .45 had not been modified since 1926.

The pistol weighed three pounds and had such a powerful recoil that it took considerable arm strength to aim it steadily and fire it accurately. Further, it had always had a tendency to fire at odd times. General Patton refused to carry one after an incident in which he stamped his foot angrily and creased his thigh when his .45 went off in its holster.

As if all this weren't enough to justify change, there were also issues of standardization and convenience. Other NATO countries had agreed on the more modern 9mm pistol, and it made good sense for the U.S. Army to use the same weapons and ammunition. The Air Force and the Navy had also already abandoned the Colt .45 and were eager for the Army to make supply easier and cheaper by doing the same.

It wasn't as though the Pentagon were rushing into the change either. It had begun to lobby for a more modern handgun back in the 1950s, and its present campaign to replace the .45 dated back to 1979. But it was only in 1985 that the decision to change handguns was finally made—not because the case for the change was not clear, but because the Colt .45 was an integral part of the world of the career army officer.

That world was a world of men, to begin with, and it was a world of American supremacy. The argument that the Army's more than 80,000 women had a very hard time with the .45 was, one suspects, more of an argument in favor of keeping the weapon than of giving it up. So, too, was the fact that the NATO countries were already using the 9mm, for that made it likely (as did in fact happen) that a

---

* References for facts and quotations used in the text will be found in the Notes section beginning on page 205. Wherever an asterisk appears in the pages that follow, there is a footnote, referenced by page number, in the back of the book.

European design, not an American one, would be chosen for the new pistol. Finally, there was the Colt name, a reminder of the world of frontier law and order. As James Sullivan, a small-arms designer, commented to a *Wall Street Journal* reporter, "Soldiers are cowboys at heart."

Even if the inability to accept such overwhelming logic had not made it clear that it was more than a weapon that was being defended, the nature of the defenders' arguments was enough to give anyone familiar with organizational change the clue that it was a whole world that was at stake. With a wonderful twist of logic, a Marine Corps veteran who helped to develop the two-handed style of pistol shooting wrote to Secretary of Defense Caspar Weinberger, "The pistol isn't of much good for modern warfare so we don't need a new one." And, when Air Force tests demonstrated that the .45 didn't operate well under adverse conditions, the Army claimed that the tests were invalid because "non-standard military mud" had been used.

The point is that the world of the army professional has been deeply undermined in the past forty years: wars that politicians wouldn't let them "win," new high-tech weaponry that shifted personnel needs from brawn to brains, the growing presence and increasing importance of women, and the necessity of treating NATO allies as equals. Perhaps most difficult of all was a shift from being seen as protectors of the peace to being seen as threats to the peace.

The Colt .45 was the symbol of a rapidly disappearing world, and to let go of it was to admit that that world was gone. If someone had argued that the career army men were reacting to the Colt .45 affair as though it were the end of the world, they might well have replied, "Damned right!" Because it was.†

There are ways of getting past such resistance and bringing about real and lasting changes that honor both the intent of their initiators and the desire of those affected to protect the integrity of their worlds. They begin with an understanding of organizational change itself and what it does to people, and they are not simple or quick to initiate. But they are being carried out by farsighted organizations

† Now the change has been snagged again, this time by members of Congress whose constituents manufacture the Colt. Even change itself won't stay put these days!

today, and it is to bring these ways of accomplishing change into wider circulation that this book has been written.

In the writing of this book, many people have been extremely helpful—some consciously and some unwittingly. The latter group is largely made up of employees, some of whose names I never learned, in the organizations where I have been working. In telling me what was going on and what it was doing to their lives and careers, they taught me most of what I know about what really happens in an organization when there is a merger or a new boss or a layoff or a departmental reorganization. They were my real teachers, for again and again they made me rethink my assumptions about change and how it can best be managed. Because we usually talked in confidence, I have identified neither them nor their organizations. That sometimes makes for vagueness, for it leads me to speak of "the vice-president of a large food-processing company" or "a supervisor at an aerospace company" rather than giving names. I apologize for the circumlocution, but I cannot in good conscience be more specific.

I have also had the help of people who more consciously guided my efforts, providing me with material from their experience and influencing my thinking through theories of their own. They include Anthony Athos, Robert Boyle, James and Elizabeth Bugental, Budd Carr, Sandi Cheldelin, Robert Cowls, Charles DeRidder, Roy Dunlap, Terry Elledge, Robert H. Hood, Jr., Chuck House, Carol Humple, Don Hutchinson, John Levy, Charles Lofy, William Livingston, Mary Luttrell, Bryan McCarthy, Donald Michael, Bud Phillips, Gene Rice, Glenn Smyth, William Swanson, Robert Tannenbaum, Thomas Ucko, and Lee Weinstein.

In the writing and publication of the book itself, another group of people were instrumental. My agents, Liz and Jim Trupin, helped me to define the project and find a publisher that understood its significance; as always they were reassuring in their faith that I could write the book I intended. My editor at Doubleday, Nick Bakalar, steered me from project to finished product, and kept challenging me to go beyond expression to communication. And my wife, Mondi, nudged and nurtured me along, rescuing me from both discouragement and grandiosity, and helping me to manage the difficult transitions in my own life.

My three children are just setting forth on their own in this world that the book describes. They and the rest of their generation are the ones who were born to this time of turmoil, and I watch them with both concern and admiration. Anne, Sarah, and Margaret—I dedicate the book to you.

PART ONE

THE CHANGE EPIDEMIC

1: Chaos in the Workplace

I have it on good authority that Delta is buying Eastern. Eastern is buying Pan Am. Pan Am is really going after United now
that it has all of United's cash, and America's Bob Crandall,
who has been devilishly silent all along, is getting ready to make
a tender offer for the whole industry once he reaches agreement
with the pilots. Furthermore, I spoke to [airline merger-maker]
Frank Lorenzo this morning, and he assured me his next targets
are Peru and Bolivia, which he plans to merge into the first low-
cost country.

Salomon Brothers analyst Julius Maldutis[*]

Diseases always attack men when they are exposed to a change.
Herodotus, *History,* fifth century B.C.

Change has always been a disruptive force in human affairs, but its
effects have never been so widespread, continuous, and deep as they
are today. We live in an overnight society where organizations appear and disappear like toadstools. Yesterday's start-up company is
one of today's Fortune 500, while yesterday's giant is shrinking and
struggling to stay alive. In the midst of such expansion and contrac-
tion, reorganization is an almost constant fact of organizational life.

But it is not just changes in size that keep our organizations in
turmoil. The marketplace and the sources of funding keep changing, and organizations keep having to reorient and restructure
themselves to deal with the new realities of economic life. USX is
struggling to transform itself from a steel company into something
else that is not yet quite clear. In the process, the solution to one
problem creates a new problem—it buys Marathon Oil and diversi-
fies thereby from one endangered industry into another. General
Motors sets out to become a new kind of an automaker and buys
Electronic Data Systems to give it the necessary information-processing capability. That acquisition triggers off a string of technical

and social changes that were unforeseen in the beginning and will surely continue for some time. The latest is the forced departure of EDS founder H. Ross Perot—although I hesitate to mention it because by the time you read this, Perot's departure may have been undone by later changes.

There are, as in GM's case, frequent struggles between the old leaders and their internal critics. When the critics win out, they introduce new visions of the future and new strategic plans; they cause further changes. Iacocca at Chrysler, Welch at GE, Olson at AT&T, and hundreds of less visible CEOs are out to change everything from their organization's relationship with its unions to their basic products and services, their organizational structures to their very cultures.

Meanwhile, even the advice about how an organization should be structured and run is changing. Corporations, government agencies, and nonprofit institutions alike are being counseled that today's successful organizations are entrepreneurial. This advice is being taken to heart not only by profit-making companies but also by hospitals and universities, where employees are being asked to look for new or unfilled niches in the marketplace and to develop new services to respond to them. And those employees who were once judged on the client service they delivered, are often now being judged on their speed, output, and economy.

The same pressures to produce are leading most organizations to begin to automate their offices, their production lines, and their warehousing facilities. Invariably they find that automation is not a self-contained change, but that it leads to far-reaching changes in how work is scheduled, assigned, and done. Automation, like other significant changes, always leads to reorganization.

There is hardly a large corporation in the country that is not trying to reduce the levels of its management structure: Union Carbide, Ford, Du Pont, Polaroid, GM, AT&T, and Exxon are only some of the more visible. Government agencies, under pressure from Gramm-Rudman and other economy efforts, are making similar efforts. At the same time, many of these organizations are also changing the way they function by decentralizing decision making. When they do this, they put authority and responsibility for far-reaching decisions in the hands of people who only recently were being told to take their orders from above. Again, change breeds change.

At the same time mergers and acquisitions are changing the structure of the organizational world. GE gets RCA, Texas Air takes over Eastern, Burroughs acquires Sperry, and Allied and Signal merge. The hundred biggest mergers in 1984 affected four and a half million workers, and the number of mergers rose 18 percent in 1985. Between 1983 and 1987, more than 12,000 companies and corporate divisions changed hands. The reorganization that follows such changes is little less than the formation of a whole new company, and in a big merger or acquisition the resulting redundancies can cause tens of thousands of employees to lose their jobs.

These mergers and acquisitions, together with the redefinition of corporate strategy that often accompanies them, lead to the divestiture of business units that don't fit in anymore. Bumble Bee Seafoods is set adrift by Castle & Cooke, Pacific Stereo cut loose from CBS, Weirton Steel unhooked from National Steel Co. Whole new conglomerates can be created by divestiture, as happened when a collection of unwanted businesses was swept together under the banner of The Henley Group after the Allied-Signal merger. "Reorganization" is too mild a term for such undertakings, which are often more like collective death-and-rebirth experiences.

In the intensely competitive marketplace, the race to develop new products and services is so constant that even companies that have not been known for their new products are developing them very fast. Campbell Soup, for example, which had gone for years with hardly any new products, has introduced 392 in the past five years. To do that takes reorganization, of course. And there are reorganizations when a product line is abandoned. In some cases, it is much more than a product line, for when Singer stopped making sewing machines, American Can Company stopped making cans, or International Harvester (no, wait, another change: "Navistar") stopped making tractors, those companies' very natures and identities were given up as well.

Liability insurance rates soar or coverage is canceled completely, and doctors, toxic-waste cleanup companies, cities, ski areas, and day-care centers are faced with changes that threaten their very existence. The liability situation is only one result of judicial and legislative changes, which have produced a mass of other change-producing regulations.

Then there is deregulation. The airlines have been on a roller coaster ever since they were deregulated. Some have been swallowed up, some have gone into bankruptcy, and others have been created—a few of which subsequently were swallowed up or went into bankruptcy. The results have been chaotic—big cities got more service than they needed, and many small cities lost the service they had previously had. Governmental changes have produced organizational changes that in turn have produced social changes. And everyone has had to reorganize to deal with the results.

Banking too has been transformed by deregulation. In New York, Bankers Trust Company sold off its branch system and recruited a staff of Wall Street traders in an effort to become a "merchant bank." Chemical Bank is staking its future on an attempt to be the first successful home banking system. Manufacturers Hanover Trust Co. shifted its focus from lending to the big blue-chip companies to supplying smaller companies with capital. In the West, Wells Fargo tightened its operational belt, thrived, and bought Crocker Bank, while Bank of America shot itself in both feet and announced that it was quite capable of bleeding to death without any outside help, thank you. First Interstate disagreed, and marshaled its forces to try to take over B of A, a move that would change not only those two large organizations but the banking business as well. Meanwhile, with all sorts of organizations now offering checking accounts, charge cards, and loans, the very concept of *bank* is changing.

The solutions offered by the experts to change-generated problems turn out to involve a great deal of change themselves. Take Quality Control, a common prescription in these days when American manufacturing is playing catch-up to the Japanese.* Hundreds of American companies have brought in experts like Deming or Juran to show them how to reduce the number of defective items coming off their production lines. But it usually turns out that you can't just "improve the quality" by a series of discrete steps that leave the rest of the organization untouched. Instead, you find yourself redesigning products and retraining production workers and revising evaluation and promotion procedures and reorganizing the company communications system. You may even begin decentralizing authority to put power in the hands of those who best know the actual production process or the needs of the customer. And when you do that, you find that you have also undermined the staff units that used to have the power to make centralized decisions. Before you are done, you may well be reorganizing the whole company.

Change would be easier to manage if we knew where it was headed, but everyone has a different picture of what the future is going to demand. John Naisbitt tells us about the ten trends that are remaking our society and its institutions and urges us to go with their flow. Gifford Pinchot recommends that we develop "intrapreneurs" within our corporations. William Ouichi says that we'd better change to Theory Z structures and methods. Peters and Waterman tell us that we all have to get closer to our customers and clients, develop a bias for action, and do seven other things that are *excellent.*

In all this conflicting advice, it is easy to miss one very constant message: Whoever is right about the shape of the future and about which strategies will best capitalize on today's changes, organizations are going to have to continue to change rapidly and radically. Tomorrow's successful organizations in every field are going to be the ones that are learning how to deal successfully with continual change today.

To be preoccupied with the content of merger and layoff and automation is to miss the pattern that they all share—that of profound organizational change. To be so distracted is to be like the gate guard who kept searching for stolen goods in the saddlebags of a thief who, night after night, rode a horse out of the emperor's palace—only to discover when it was too late that the man had been stealing horses. It is not this or that change which we need to attend to but change itself.

The outcome of our preoccupation with content is that we plan and manage the technical, economic, and staffing aspects of organizational changes—the divestiture, let us say—with great care. But we do not foresee or know what to do with the psychological effects of change on people. We are unprepared when the changes we make disorient people and leave them demoralized, self-absorbed, and full of mistrust. We are surprised when we set out to improve productivity with a new technique, only to find that productivity falls because of the disruptions caused by its introduction. In the end, the very goals of the changes on which the organization's future depends are often threatened by the effects of the changes on the people who must carry them out. We encounter resistance to the changes, which slows down their implementation, increases their cost, and may in the end force them to be abandoned.

On February 11, 1986, Wells Fargo Bank announced its plan to purchase Crocker National Bank. Crocker employees learned of it in the morning news. It was the more difficult for them to assimilate because only a few years earlier their bank had been bought by a British bank, and the changes following upon that acquisition had been far-reaching and painful.

A few hours after the media broke the story, the following scene took place in San Francisco's financial district, where a Crocker building and a Wells Fargo building face one another across Montgomery Street.* In the window of a third-floor office, some Crocker employees put up a large sign reading APPLAUSE! Across the way, Wells Fargo employees responded with a sign reading WELCOME! A few minutes later the Crocker sign was replaced with one reading CAREER OPPORTUNITIES? This time the reply took much longer; the Wells Fargo employees finally taped up a sign without any words on it—only a large question mark.

This is more than office horseplay; it is a small example of the effects of change on employees. The prognosis for the employees of acquired companies is not very good. Of the thirty-four top officers and directors of Gulf Oil at the time of its merger with Chevron, only three were still employed there eighteen months later. About half of Gulf's 41,000 total work force left during the same period. Other significant changes can have similar effects. Thirty out of Beatrice Company's thirty-eight top operating officers either quit or were fired during the wave of changes that Chairman James L. Dutt brought about.*

The effects of change go far beyond the loss of actual jobs. Mergers, changes in leadership, and reorientations in strategy begin avalanches of secondary and tertiary changes that may include spinoffs of unwanted businesses, redefinitions of corporate goals, geographical consolidations, and changes in products or services. Any one of these shifts alone would be the source of considerable distress and disruption within an organization. Taken as a whole, they can leave an organization in chaos. Presumably, each of the changes made sense in traditional business terms, but the executives who decided to make them would have done well to consider the psychological impact of change.

Andrew C. Sigler, the chairman of Champion International, understands what change does to people. Looking back at his company's acquisition of St. Regis Corporation, which made it the largest American paper company, he said, "The people trauma in this whole process almost guarantees that there won't be a productivity increase for a considerable period of time. Until the cuts have been made, people sit around and talk. That's all they do. They're scared to death."*

He might have added that even after the cuts are made, the scars remain. The same amount of work must be done by fewer workers, who are overwhelmed by the task they face and confused by how unclear roles become when everyone is taking on new duties. Stress and ambiguity are compounded by the "survivor's syndrome." At most organizations where big work-force cuts have been made, those who remain feel guilty and anxious. The guilt comes from the mysterious way in which some make it through a change and some do not. (The survivors ask, "Why did I make it, while the others didn't? Did I sell out in some way? Am I responsible for my friends losing their jobs?") The anxiety comes from waiting for the other shoe to fall. ("When's it going to happen to me? The others didn't get any warning, and I won't either.") Managers, who expect the "survivors" to be grateful, are usually caught unprepared by these reactions. And not understanding them, such managers usually make the mistake of treating them as signs of disloyalty, ingratitude, or poor motivation.

Ironically, the very organizations that hire outplacement services to assist terminated employees in getting their careers back on track and their lives back together often forget the trauma of those who remain. This is disastrously shortsighted, for the casualties who remain do the organization far more damage than the casualties who leave. How can organizational leaders and managers so often overlook that fact? How can they thereby jeopardize the very changes on which their organization's survival depends? The answer to these questions uncovers a blind spot in our view of change that is difficult to recognize because it is built right into our culture.

Change has long been a part of the American story. In some ways it is *the* American story. It was not simply that there was so much change going on in this new and rapidly developing country—though that was important—as it was that a whole new attitude toward change had been created, an attitude which transformed change from an often uncomfortable fact of life into a positive good. On his visit to America a hundred and fifty years ago, Alexis de Tocqueville noted in his diary:

> Born often under another sky, placed in the middle of an always moving scene, himself driven by the irresistible torrent which draws all about him, the American has no time to tie himself to anything. He grows accustomed only to change, and ends by regarding it as the natural state of man. He feels the need of it, more, he loves it; for the instability, instead of meaning disaster to him, seems to give birth only to miracles all about him.*

To be ready and able to change has always been the prerequisite for success in America. This belief in the positive value of change has always impressed and dismayed people from older and more stable societies, where the status quo was a valuable heritage and it was *change* that needed to be justified. In those societies tradition acted as a brake on change, so people could assimilate social and organizational changes more slowly.

In America, the status quo has always been seen as merely the product of past changes, and it was resistance to further changes that demanded justification. To be unable or unready to change with the times was not just a private misfortune. It was looked upon as little less than a socially and organizationally subversive condition. The result was that Americans have always found themselves in the ironic position of endorsing the very changes that are undermining their lives. In that crazy paradox, Americans have always been uniquely handicapped when it came to understanding what change was really doing to their society, their organizations, and themselves.

This paradox, so basic to the American experience, has made it very difficult for our leaders and managers to appreciate the human effects of the changes that they initiate. It has even made it hard for them to appreciate the impact of such changes on themselves. In the companies and public institutions where I have been a consultant, such men and women often apologize to me about the anxiety they feel at the prospect of the changes they are creating. They not only saw off the limb they are sitting on, but they blame themselves because they believe that their anxieties are signs of personal weakness. Their official view is that if change is necessary and explained carefully, we all ought to be able to handle it.

Perhaps that was so twenty-five or thirty years ago, when most of our leaders and middle managers were learning their business. The fact is that, for many reasons, change today hits people much harder than it did then. For one thing, changes are increasingly frequent today, and as we will see in the next chapter, the process through which people must pass to reorient themselves to a changed situation takes time. When changes snowball, they begin to overlap and people get stuck in a state of constant transition. A department head in an insurance company where this had happened described the result as "people dashing around, lost and frightened, like dogs on a freeway."

The frequency of change is fed by a number of factors. One is the rush to use technological change for competitive advantage—the sense that you can't afford any longer *not* to change when there is an opportunity and a potential gain in doing so. McGraw-Hill, for example, used to be organized by media, with books, magazines, and statistical services as separate divisions. But with electronics and computers making instantaneous "publication" possible, that whole publishing empire has been reorganized into nineteen "market focus groups" that are charged with the task of getting information rapidly to different trades and professions. "We believed that the market for information was going to change, and if we were going to participate, we would have to master the new technologies," explained CEO Joseph Dionne. A *Fortune* reporter who studied the result, however, reported that the changes "have thrown the company into turmoil." The publications company, the former home of sixty-one magazines and newsletters, has been dismantled and those publications are now scattered through eight "market focus groups." More than a dozen high-ranking managers have left because of the changes, including such important people as the editors and advertising sales managers of both *Business Week* and the computer magazine *Byte*. Ten percent of the professional staff of the McGraw-Hill forecasting unit, Data Resources, Inc., left as well.*

Another reason for the increased frequency of change is the very "market-driven" quality that is so often prescribed as essential to success in today's organizational world. Yesterday's companies developed new products and abandoned old ones at a relatively slow pace, but today's producers have linked themselves to public interests and tastes that can change overnight. That responsiveness aggravates the problem by setting up a feedback circuit that amplifies change, so the way that organizations seek to profit from change makes the problem of change more severe.

An example: For years, a couple of companies manufactured sneakers for a wide range of athletic and recreational activities, but the jogging craze changed the whole business and created a large number of new companies, some of which grew rapidly. But now the same forces that created those companies have created a new group of successors, as aerobics begins to rival jogging as the fitness preference. So Nike Inc. plateaus out and Reebok International takes off. But the river of change continues to flow, and Reebok too has begun to lose some of its ground to competitors that are temporarily more attuned to the market's demand of the moment.

Today's world is changing so quickly and constantly that even the study of change itself changes. Earlier this year I prepared some materials for a presentation to the executive management team at a large aerospace company. Wanting some graphic material, I cut out a *New Yorker* cartoon that showed a woman chiding a very sedentary-looking man: "If Coca-Cola can change after all these years, why can't you?" But in the ten days between putting the material together and using it in the management program, Coca-Cola changed again, and the joke was on me.

The accelerated product cycles and the technological changes have combined with the increasingly competitive nature of the marketplace to create still another factor that has increased the frequency of organizational change. Traditional methods of developing new products and services are often frustratingly slow, and so today's organizational leaders are tempted to acquire organizations that already do what they would like to be able to do. This leads to a "speculator mentality" among organizational leaders and fuels today's brisk market in merger and acquisition.

Even resisting that tide can trigger off significant changes, as when Union Carbide unloaded such stable and successful product lines as Eveready Batteries, Prestone Antifreeze, and Glad Bags in its efforts to foil GAF's attempted takeover; and Phillips Petroleum sold off $2 billion in assets to finance the rebuff of T. Boone Pickens's unfriendly advances.

The picking up and dropping of small units by big ones undermines the sense that change happens for reasons that have anything to do with actual worth or performance. When Bill Sanko, the head of a GTE division that made telephone transmission products, met with the corporate officers in 1984, he announced proudly that (1) his new division had just begun to make money for GTE, (2) it had gained more customers than predicted, and, (3) it had done it with less money than expected. They thanked him and informed him that the division didn't fit in with their plans anymore, so they were going to get rid of it. Sanko's response was understated, to say the least: "There was a sense of disappointment for us. All of us had put a lot into it."* People affected by such decisions easily grow cynical about their corporation's concern for them and what they are trying to do.

Changes are more disruptive today because they are likelier than in the past to have an all-or-nothing quality about them. It is increasingly difficult to try out changes on a small scale, for, as Abernathy, Clark, and Kantrow have noted in their *Industrial Renaissance,* management must move from idea to full-scale implementation without the dozens of little delays and reorientations that gave people time to get comfortable with the change. There is, they write, "no relaxed breathing space for managers to rethink their course. There is, instead, the competitive necessity of making relatively major changes in products and processes without seriously interrupting the flow of goods to the market."*

Separating out cause and effect in these matters is impossible, but there is a definite connection between the cumulative effect of these all-or-nothing changes (made increasingly frequently, for reasons that often have little to do with performance) and a growing alienation of the work force from the interests of the organization. In the days when today's senior managers were learning their trade, employee disaffection was largely confined to the parts of the work force that did very heavy, dull work or to those whose working conditions were substandard. (One used to hear about foreign objects occasionally welded into the hollows of Detroit autos, forever to rumble and rattle beyond the reach of conventional repair.)

But today's chronic absenteeism, widespread employee theft, and carelessness about quality are not limited to exploited blue-collar workers. I recall the vice-president of a medium-sized bank, for example, who admitted that he got almost nothing done on Fridays: "In my mind, I'm already out with my family on my boat," he explained. Opinion Research Corporation has kept records of employee ratings of their companies' management for the past fifteen years, and those ratings have fallen markedly. In the early seventies, 70 percent of the managers gave favorable ratings, but by the early eighties less than 50 percent did.*

If all of this were not enough reason for organizational leadership to be concerned with the impact of change, there is also the enormously expanded concept of organizational liability. As product liability, it is often the source of significant change—witness the bankruptcies of asbestos-products maker Johns Manville, and A. H. Robins, the developer of the Dalkon Shield. Even where the product or service is not at risk from the new liabilities, the organization is affected by them because it is far more likely to be sued by its own employees than it once was. Typically these suits, about age and sex discrimination, stress-related illnesses, or unfair terminations, come from employees in change-related situations. In California, job-related stress cases have more than quintupled in the past seven years, while total worker's compensation cases have risen by only 13 percent during the same period.* Yesterday's managers could make their staff changes without much concern for these matters. Today's managers cannot.

Yet old attitudes, even such obviously self-defeating ones, die slowly. I recently gave a briefing to the top personnel executives at a corporation that regularly appears on *Fortune*'s "Best Managed Companies" list. The younger personnel officers nodded and glanced knowingly at one another as I talked about the impacts of change on employees. When I finished, however, their sixtyish boss thanked me but said he guessed that he was too old-fashioned to take the approach I was recommending. "I believe that you just figure out what has to be done and tell them what you expect them to do. The good ones will do it!"

The commanders of the Light Brigade ("Theirs not to reason why,/Theirs but to do and die!") worked on the same principle. The results were not very good then and they are even less likely to be good now.

If management must take the blame for such stupidity, organizational consultants must share it. They have thumped on organizational chests, peered down corporate throats, listened to the institutional symptoms, and written their prescriptions without sufficient sensitivity to what the changes they prescribe will do to those affected. I listen even today to such people at their professional meetings talking about being "change agents" and "unfreezing stuck organizations." I hear facile contrasts between organizations that are past-oriented and static and those that are future-oriented and dynamic. I read studies of resistance to change that suggest that it comes from a failure to share the vision or from a selfish attachment to the personal benefits of the status quo—or, worse yet, from a rigid and neurotic personality.

But the resistance to change is not an inherently pathological condition. More often than not, it is simply a defense of the person's own reality. As the English social scientist Donald Schon points out, being part of an organizational status quo "provides a focus for loyalty, a definition of role . . . an upward path through which progress and promotion are defined, and a perspective on the world."* This is why the usual approaches to dealing with resistance, which emphasize information and persuasion, so often fail to reach the mark.

Yet we keep acting as though more information would bring people around. It did not bring Detroit executives around when their auto companies were losing ground to small foreign imports. It did not bring around the owner of a small plumbing equipment company that I visited, who canceled a personally advantageous pension plan because it would have required him to "give away pensions" to employees too. It did not bring around the army officers who wanted to retain the Colt .45.

We also keep acting as though a clear understanding of where change is headed is enough to get us there. We are such a future-oriented society that we spend our energies arguing about destinations and forgetting the journey, though it is the journey that will make us whatever we become. Long before they can come to pass, our predicted futures are outmoded by new changes. Looking back, yesterday's predictions read like the old *Popular Science* stories about how we'd all be flying autogyros to work by 1975. In spite of that, we delude ourselves into thinking that if we have some clear destination in mind—or at least understand why we are in transition and can see some advantage to the journey—we will have only minor difficulties en route.

But that is simply not so. Organizational charts change so often today that they have to be written in pencil. People are laid off by bosses who themselves are laid off in the next round of "downsizing." Yesterday's manufacturer is today an importer of finished products and simply adds its name to them. But then tomorrow one of its former suppliers emerges from nowhere as the unexpected competitor that takes away all its business. Just when people think they know where they stand, interest rates rise or the dollar falls, and the ground caves in under them.

We need to let go of the fantasy that once the current storms of change are past we'll have clear sailing. It is rough seas as far as the eye can see, and we are simply going to have to learn to navigate them. We are going to have to learn to manage the human effects of organizational change and what people thus affected can do, in turn, to an organization. As Harvard's well-known organizational psychologist, Harry Levinson, said recently, "The most critical problem executives have is that they don't understand the powerful impact of change on people. Employees get badly bruised, but the attitude is, 'Oh well, they'll get over it.' "* In a competitive marketplace where organizations no longer operate with yesterday's comfortable margins, that attitude is an unaffordable luxury.

2: *Unmanaged Transition and Unmanageable Change*

> We trained hard . . . but every time we were beginning to form up into teams, we would be reorganized. I was to learn later in life that we tend to meet any new situation by reorganizing . . . and a wonderful method it can be of creating the illusion of progress while producing inefficiency and demoralization.
>
> Petronius Satyricon, First century A.D.

Anyone who has ever tried to reorganize an office, a department, or a whole company knows about "resistance"—what most people refer to unthinkingly as "resistance to change." Yet what people usually have in mind is really resistance to *transition,* not to change. The difference between the two is not generally understood, but it is important, particularly to leaders and managers who are trying to change how their organizations work.*

Change occurs when something new starts or something old stops, and it takes place at a particular point in time. But *transition* cannot be localized in time that way, since it is the gradual psychological process through which individuals and groups reorient themselves so that they can function and find meaning in a changed situation. Change often starts with a new beginning, but transition must start with an ending—with people letting go of old attitudes and behaviors.

Changes require people to make transitions, and it is these necessary transitions rather than the changes themselves that are difficult. Consider the relation between change and transition in the situation recently faced by Macy's California, the twenty-five-store western division of the R. H. Macy & Co. chain.* Macy's was for a long time the class act among California department stores, and a very profitable one at that. But then the retail market in California began to change. Upscale operations like Neiman-Marcus and Nordstrom's crowded Macy's from one side, while discount stores crowded them from the other. Macy's sales totals flattened out while those of several rival chains continued to climb, and its profits actually began to fall. External changes clearly called for internal changes.

A new CEO was brought in and he brought with him a new style and a new plan. His predecessor had run what one former Macy's executive called "an open society," while the new CEO intimidated people. Partisans of one man or the other argued over which style was better, but the fact was that there had been a significant change. The new plan required other fundamental changes, particularly in its new emphasis on customer service. In the past, Macy's had been a more or less self-service operation, and salespeople had been instructed to stay at the registers and ring up purchases. They could even be disciplined if they left to help a customer on the floor. But with the change to "customer service," they had to let go of their familiar way of doing things. As a result of the policy change, they could now be disciplined for not going out on the floor to help a customer, and the transition was difficult. A measure of the difficulty was the 223 percent rise in grievances filed by sales, stockroom, and marketing workers in the year following the change. The lesson: When people have to let go of their old ways of dealing with the world, they feel threatened and are likely to strike back at whomever they take to be responsible for their loss.

Another example: In a food-processing plant where I served as a consultant, they changed the stockroom and the procedures for using it. Formerly it had been a large, open room, where supervisors could smoke during breaks; the stockroom shelves had been accessible to these supervisors, who kept personal caches of replacement parts on them; inventories were made periodically by a clerk, who always found that a great many parts were unaccounted for; with a dozen private caches and constant losses, spare-parts costs ran high, and with so little inventory control they sometimes ran out of parts —which, in turn, reinforced the supervisors' tendency to hoard private supplies of the parts.

The changes were meant to save money and keep track of parts.

A computer was installed, access to the shelves was blocked by a new counter, and the private caches of parts were merged into a single, well-arranged stock. Finally, the seating space was sacrificed for new shelving. Result: The problems were solved, but the supervisors experienced the ending of their old power as so traumatic that they found ways to make the new system almost unworkable, and it was not until a new stockroom specialist was hired and the facility put under a different manager—at an unforeseen additional cost of time and money—that the change began to work. The increased cost was several months and thousands of dollars. The lesson: Unmanaged transitions are likely to lead to unmanageable changes.

Organizations are constantly transferring people from one setting to another, and expecting the changes to work without much sense of how difficult the transition can be. Whenever I think of that situation, I remember a college professor I once knew who had taught briefly at Harvard while he was studying there for his doctorate. But he failed to get a regular job there, so he left for a smaller and less prestigious college. At his new teaching position, he always gave two grades on every paper: the first, the grade it received; and the second, the grade it would have received at Harvard. Needless to say, he was not very successful in his new organizational assignment. The lesson: At bottom, it is a person's identity that he or she has trouble letting go of, and it is that identity that stands in the way of the change producing its desired result.

As a final example of the failure to see that change requires transition, consider Xerox, which made a change two years ago to the currently fashionable "just in time" inventory principle, perfected by the Japanese.* Under that principle a company keeps no more than a few days' (sometimes only a few hours') materials on hand, and in the process it saves a good deal of money. Xerox planned the new procedures with great care, but the company was less successful in foreseeing and managing a string of transitions that the new procedures created, outside as well as inside the corporation.

All Xerox's gains in lower inventories were experienced as losses (increased inventories) by its suppliers, who were now expected to hold materials until the manufacturer was ready for them. To make matters worse, the whole system depended on suppliers being ready to respond instantly to the manufacturer's orders, and that put them under the big company's thumb in a way that they had never been before. Add to all this the fact that "just in time" inventories were part of a larger change in which Xerox traded longer contracts for higher-quality levels in parts, and you can see that Xerox's "new procedure" was a change that forced the suppliers into transitions in which they would have to give up a great deal of autonomy.

Xerox congratulated itself on the gains, but as the suppliers began to discover what they had lost in the bargain, new problems arose. Their bulging inventories caused them to cut back production and to resist requests to produce new parts when the old ones sat unsold on their shelves. In the end, their problems became Xerox's as well, for the effects of the problems showed up in delays in the Xerox production line.

As often happens when organizational planning overlooks the transition process, Xerox had to undertake a second planning effort and make a whole further round of changes to deal with the transitions caused by the first changes. Fortunately the situation had not deteriorated too far, and the second round of changes worked. Production was reorganized so that with more predictable requirements, suppliers could plan their output better. As it became clear how deeply Xerox's changes affected its suppliers, the big company took on the responsibility for helping the smaller companies train their own personnel to let go of the old ways and begin doing things in the new ways.

The second round of changes made the transitions easier to bear at the supplier level. Some suppliers began to thrive in the new environment. One company, with Xerox's help, cut its manufacturing time on one important part from three and a half weeks to one day. That company has been so changed by its experience that it has started working with *its* suppliers to make similar changes in their production, inventory, and distribution.

The lesson: Change begets change, and at every step people are plunged into transition; it is only if you can foresee those transitions and foresee who is likely to lose something that you will be in a position to manage successfully the loss, the transition, and ultimately the change itself. To say that there isn't time to plan or carry out all this is simply to say that because there isn't time to do it right now, there is going to have to be time to do it wrong now and then right later—a dubious economy.

Change and transition differ in another way. In a change, the new can replace the old immediately. Bosses, machines, company names, and policies can be changed overnight. But in transition there is a prolonged no-man's-land between the old reality and the new one. In this in-between time neither the old rules nor the new rules work, even though one or the other may be officially in place. It is a time when everything feels up in the air, chaotic, unreal, confused, empty, meaningless. I call this time (or time-out) the "neutral zone."

In a recent Organizational Transition Seminar, one of the participants said that he could recognize the neutral zone in his personal life but he wasn't sure what it looked like in an organization. All at once half a dozen people were talking: The human resources director of one of California's largest real estate companies told about a whole department in his firm where "nothing is being done—nothing!" because people are demoralized by a traumatic change in the top management; the manager of the information services department at a very large bank told about the chaos produced by procedural changes that half of the department implemented and half didn't; the president of a half-billion-dollar-a-year conglomerate told about the struggle within the corporation between those who wanted to rush forward into an unplanned future and those who wanted to go back to a past that was irrevocably lost.

The lesson provided by such cases is that it is not enough to define the objective that an organizational change is meant to achieve and explain the plan for getting there. Managing the ending that such a change will entail is essential, but it still leaves out an important aspect of transition management: a way to shepherd people through this ambiguous gap between an old world and a new one. As every neutral-zone leader since Moses has found, that wilderness is bigger and more confusing than any map would lead one to believe.

Transition is a three-phase process that culminates in a new beginning. Change can start with something new, but in the psychological process of transition, the beginning comes last. It is only after the ground has been cleared and has lain fallow for a time that the new growth can appear. In a sense, therefore, the secret of managing a new beginning is to manage well the ending and the neutral zone that must precede it.

But there is more to this third phase of Transition Management than that, because a genuinely new beginning is a frustratingly ambiguous combination of planning carefully and resisting the temptation to overplan. To read the management literature, one would think that new beginnings were made in a conscious and rational sense, like moves in a chess match. But anyone who studies actual innovations and times of renewal will discover that there is a large element of unpredictability about them. The English novelist John Galsworthy was on the mark when he wrote, ". . . the beginnings . . . of all human undertakings are untidy."*

A moment of reflection on your own life will show how often even the most significant new beginnings are "accidental." You bumped into an old friend, who told you about another friend who was looking for someone to help with . . . and you got the job that you'd been looking for for over a year. You met your spouse at a party that you didn't really want to go to, and your first impression of this person who became your partner for life was that he or she wasn't anything out of the ordinary. Whatever clarity of shape such beginnings possess is usually only definable in retrospect.

Many new technical beginnings are similarly inauspicious. Vulcanized rubber, artificial fabric fibers, and a host of other technical breakthroughs originated as mistakes of one sort or another. Archimedes discovered how to measure the volume of irregular objects in his bathtub, and Kekule first understood molecular constitution during a bus ride through the deserted streets of nighttime London. The pacemaker was conceived during an unsuccessful operation on a dog, when the doctor accidentally brushed the animal's failing heart with an electric probe. Pasteur's great work with infectious diseases began with a study of the role of bacteria in fermentation, which began in turn with some tartrate solution that had accidentally turned moldy. (That interest in tartrate began with Pasteur's study under a crystallographer at the École Normale in Paris, who had been the favorite pupil of Abbé René Juste Haüy—who had originally discovered the nature of crystalline structure when he accidentally made the embarrassing mistake of dropping and breaking a prismatic crystal belonging to a friend.)*

The literature on creativity and innovation is full of such examples. Their point is not that new beginnings just happen in a random fashion but that they emerge from this strange "nowhere" that we are calling the neutral zone—and that they do so only when there is a readiness for them, which is produced by letting go of some earlier idea or situation.

Certainly people who cannot let go of an earlier answer cannot capitalize on a new one. The German scientist who discovered Novocain decided that it was going to replace general anesthetics in surgery and promoted it on that basis. Surgeons were not convinced, but dentists began to use the new substance. So fixed was the scientist's purpose, however, that he actually campaigned against the dentists' use of his discovery.*

In chapter 5 we will see that there are a good many things one can do to help a new beginning along, so I am certainly not advocating managerial passivity. I am simply saying that the new idea, like the new energy to put it into practice and the new sense of purpose based on a commitment to it, are not manufactured goods. They take shape as parts of a natural process —transition—which can be encouraged and protected but cannot be forced to happen. And it *must* be encouraged and protected, because transition is more than just an unfortunately necessary disruption of the status quo and a source of psychological distress. It is also the source of renewal and creative reorientation in all individuals and organizations.

Organizations often fail in their attempts to renew and reorient themselves because they confuse *starting* with *beginning*. The former is an essentially mechanical process that can happen any time the circumstances permit: If I have a key, I can start my car; if the participants and I are there, I can start a Transitions Seminar on time. But I cannot *start* a new phase of my life or my career so arbitrarily. To launch a whole new chapter requires a *beginning*, which is the final phase in an organic process that does not happen just because I decide that it is time. Beginnings happen when the transition process gets to the point where they are ready to happen. As the Japanese poet Ikkyu wrote in the fifteenth century:

If you break open
The cherry tree,
    Where are the flowers?
But in the springtime,
See how they bloom!

If we believe a new beginning is needed, we must attend to the transitions that are already under way in our organizations. And if we want to find the transitions, we should look at the changes that challenge us from without and within.

Ironically, one of the problems that many leaders and managers have is that they do not like to think of what they are dealing with as changes. "We're not making any changes," the manager of an oil refinery told me recently. "We're just tightening up our performance appraisal system and redefining our promotion criteria." No changes, indeed!

Technically trained people often overlook the fact that "solutions to problems" are changes. They do so partly because their technical focus is very narrow, and they have trouble seeing the larger organizational context; and they also do so because they tend to be uncomfortable with people's "irrational" reactions to their ideas, and so they try to forget such reactions whenever they can. But unless they can see that a solution is a change, that a change requires transition, and that transition must begin with somebody letting go of something, they will not be able to implement their ideas in the real world of the organization except by force.

In organization after organization that I have worked with, I have arrived to find the same situation: Changes have been planned with great care, and transitions have been completely forgotten. A large health maintenance organization put months of effort into the selection and installation of a big IBM computer to replace a mixed system of machines from different manufacturers. The new system permitted different departments to share one immense data base and greatly increased the information-processing capacity of the organization as a whole.

But no one had thought through the difficulty people would have in letting go of their old systems and the sense of competence and control that individuals had built up with the aid of those systems. No one had foreseen the resentment that other departments would feel if the greatly expanded EDP received its own vice-president. No one had thought through the impact on the company's rather informal organizational style of new, highly structured IBM procedures and the rationalistic style of training that went with them. And no one had thought through a loss of loyalty caused by an influx of new specialists whose primary loyalty was to a particular system of technology rather than to the organization. (That last problem was compounded when old-timers discovered that these new and "disloyal" employees earned more than they did, so before long everyone's loyalty began to slide.) "If we hadn't already spent $3 million on this changeover," mused one of the executives during my first visit to the company, "I'd see if we couldn't go back to the way things were."

I happen to have drawn most of these examples from physical and technological changes, but I might equally have illustrated the point with examples where personnel changes or cultural changes led to disruptive transitions. When he was president of the Parker Pen Company, William Swanson wrestled with the problem of a tyrannical manager who achieved good levels of productivity only at a heavy cost in morale. Finally he decided to reassign the man and replace him with a person who was respected and liked by most of his subordinates. Swanson was amazed when two of the transferred manager's key subordinates—who had been, he knew, miserable under their boss's dictatorial control—announced that they were considering leaving because of the change. Talking to them, he discovered something that always comes as a surprise—that even when a situation is experienced as negative, people identify with it and experience its disappearance as a loss.

This makes so little sense to many managers that they simply do not believe their eyes and ears. Or they pass the whole thing off with the conclusion that people are "basically conservative." (As an executive from a large aerospace company recently told me, "If you let them, people will hold on, white-knuckled, to the past!") Yet those phrases are too simple, and action based on them is likely to be ineffective. They are misleading because they falsely suggest that resistance to change results from selfishness or some kind of constitutional peculiarity. There are, to be sure, people who resist change out of narrow self-interest, and there are also people who resist change because they need stability so badly. But if such people were the only forces holding back organizational change, reorganizations and leadership changes and mergers would be much easier to bring off than they are.

Since change is going on around and even inside us all the time, you would think that we would be used to it. But this undeniably constant, if gradual, change is impossible to keep track of. Our minds work by organizing the vast field of our awareness into comprehensible patterns of "reality," and we hold these patterns as long as they are effective in our dealings with our worlds. To put it another way, each of us holds on to our own individual "world" as long as it works to do so—and sometimes a bit longer. Let me illustrate the point with a personal anecdote.

A couple of years ago I came out of a nursery with a bag of fertilizer on my shoulder and tried to open the back door of my green VW van, only to find it locked. Puzzling over my memory that I had left it unlocked, I went around to the sliding side door. As I put the fertilizer on the seat, I noticed a bag of empty bottles on the floor and started trying to remember if my wife had asked me to return them to the market. I walked around to the driver's door and climbed in, speculating as I did so on the possibility that I was developing an early case of Alzheimer's Disease. But before I could remember at what age its symptoms tended to be first noticeable, my eye fell on two cigarettes in the ashtray, one with lipstick on it and one without. I thought to myself that my wife had started smoking again . . . and then (worse!), that she was smoking with a man. For a moment my mind raced through all the doors of possibility opened by this evidence. Then, suddenly, I felt the stab of embarrassing enlightenment and jumped out of the van, grabbed the sack of fertilizer out of the back, looked around to see if anyone had seen my faux pas, and ran fifty feet down the line of cars in the lot to where *my* green VW van was parked.

In such situations, we can hardly believe that we cling to our worlds so resolutely in spite of signals that indicate that there is something wrong with them, or that our worlds are so completely and sometimes embarrassingly private. But all of us do live in worlds of our own, which are different in small ways or large from the worlds of those around us. Our worlds share enough character-istics so that we can talk intelligibly to one another, but at bottom, we live in worlds of meaning that are to some degree unique.

We begin to wonder about these matters as children, when we puzzle over questions like whether the green that we see looks "green" to others too. We begin to sense what "world" means when we realize that dogs see in black and white, that they hear whole ranges of sound that we cannot, and that a trail of smells is as clearly marked for them as a line of footprints is for us.

Anyone trying to deal successfully with a particular transition can only do so by trying to understand the subjective "worlds" of the people who are affected, for it is only in terms of those worlds that the pain of endings, the chaos of the neutral zone, and the excitement of new beginnings have any meaning. Whatever its con-tent, a human being's subjective world is shaped by five factors, and it is only by understanding them that leaders and managers can overcome their own natural perceptual chauvinism and know how someone else is likely to experience the transitions produced by the changes they are bringing about.

First, there is personal history, which endows events and objects with special meaning. As Mark Twain said, "A cat that's sat on a hot stove will never sit on another—nor on a cold stove, for that matter." Personal history makes some events "hot," so individual employees see the same change differently, based on their past expe-rience. The wise manager or leader will be sensitive to whatever personal history he knows about.

There is a collective history as well. Old scars, left over from previous misunderstandings and mistreatment, ache whenever a comparable situation presents itself. Managers who may themselves not even have worked for the organization when the old hurts oc-curred will not appreciate how much they still define people's pic-ture of "how we're treated." And for that reason, such managers may not discover until it is too late that their explanations of why changes were occurring or how they would be implemented are disbelieved.

In a food-processing plant where I have been consulting recently, a set of physical and technical changes that are essential to the plant's survival were widely believed to be motivated by a desire to get rid of old-timers who lacked much education. While untrue, the belief made perfect sense to people who had seen younger, better-educated people picked for promotions over the previous few years. Such criteria had never been important before, but when a new management group came in a few years before, they had begun to be. The change had never been explained to the older workers, who only knew that they had lost something—just as now, they were once again threatened with loss.

Second, there are cultural values. Things have different meanings to people from different cultures. Argument is the best way to find the truth in one culture, and it is terrible effrontery in another. The Latino employees at a factory where I helped to set up a Transition Management program are the products of a culture that places unusually high value upon maintaining relationships and group membership. These employees preferred to avoid individual recognition for fear that it would alienate their fellow workers, and often covered for one another so that weaker workers would not be disciplined. It is not, therefore, surprising that they found it very difficult to participate in designing the selection process through which some of their co-workers would be terminated by the company. The plant's Anglo managers, schooled in the techniques of participative management, were nonplussed and were at first disposed to chalk the reaction up to a "refusal to take responsibility."

Third, there is temperament or natural style, something that is not simply the product of personal experience but is, rather, an inherent way of perceiving and evaluating experience.* The Swiss psychiatrist Carl Jung noted that some people are naturally present-oriented and get their data from the details of an actual situation, while others are future-oriented and get their data from the general pattern of possibility within a situation. In times of transition, the latter group, which he called Intuitives, are likely to be excited by visions of the future—just as strategic planning theory (which is largely written by Intuitives) says that everyone will be. But the first group, which Jung called Sensates, is likely to find all that "visionary stuff" a bit unreal and to need step-by-step plans for getting from here to there.

Fourth, there is gender. Even though men and women can learn to perceive things in very similar ways, developmental psychologists suggest that there is a subtle relational cast to most women's reality and a kind of thing-in-itself cast to most men's.* A classic male-female conflict over change has the man accusing the woman of forgetting the needs of the practical situation in her concern for everyone's feelings, and the woman accusing the man of being too preoccupied with getting results to see what he is doing to people in the process.

Finally, there is life phase.* Things hold different meanings for us when we are sixteen than they do when we are sixty. One way of thinking of the cycle of human development, in fact, is as a cycle of worlds or realities. Up to a person's middle years, it usually feels as though there is another chance ahead if whatever one is doing now doesn't work out. Up to the age of forty or so, changes are not so likely to represent the end of a person's dreams. But after that point, a lateral transfer instead of an expected promotion, the loss of a boss who had one's interests at heart, or removal from a project that had personal meaning are likely to leave deep wounds that take a long time to heal. They feel like the "end of the world," because they mark the ending of the dream that gave the world its meaning.

In these five ways our personal worlds are created. Gradually those worlds undergo a natural evolution across the span of our lives. And at the same time they are constantly being reshaped by the impact of our external environments. Slowly and imperceptibly, therefore, change undermines and forces us to reorganize the pattern of meaning that we call *reality*.

Now, it may seem as though it should be possible to stay current with that change and make all the little day-by-day modifications necessary for our worlds to remain up-to-date. But we can't be changing things all the time. We have to wake up in the morning to the same world we left at night—and even more, to wake up as the same people who went to bed the night before. If there are little discrepancies between what we expect and what we actually experience, we are likely to suppress an awareness of them, since they are less important to our psychological well-being than are the big correspondences. It is, in fact, only on the basis of the ongoing continuity that we can even recognize the small changes. It is the continuity that enables us to know where we belong, where we are going—even who we are.

The fact is that the discrepancies exist, however, and that over time they are likely to get bigger. So we risk having what Gregory Bateson used to call the Boiled Frog Experience. If a frog is put into a pot of cold water and the heat is turned on under it, the water can be heated to boiling, degree by degree, without the frog's reacting to what is happening, because its skin cannot distinguish small and gradual temperature changes. In the same way there is a danger that we might drift farther and farther from actuality in our attempt to preserve our reality intact—until at last we awoke to the terror of a world that was so unintelligible that we simply could not put it back together again.

Sudden and traumatic changes do occasionally destroy people's worlds completely, but what is more likely to happen is that when their worlds get more than a little out of alignment with reality, a change jars them loose and they pop back into focus in a new way. A person moves from one department to another, gets a promotion, gets a new office mate, or is forced to learn a new role and, like the fragments of colored glass in the kaleidoscope, his or her world is jolted into a different pattern of arrangement. But although this analogy is useful, it is inexact. Unlike the kaleidoscopic rearrangements, the repatternings that go on in our minds do not take place quickly. It takes people a surprisingly long time to let go of the old pattern and then another long time in the patternless chaos of the neutral zone before they can make a new pattern their own.

No wonder they experience change as a threat! What is at stake is the very source of meaning and identity in their lives. As psychotherapists James and Elizabeth Bugental have written, "The price of preserving the familiar world and one's place in it may be literal and physical death, but that price has been paid repeatedly by men and women throughout history."* So it makes no sense to treat resistance to transition as unnatural. It is the completely natural act of self-preservation.

As the Bugentals' statement suggests, however, this natural self-preservation can also be self-destructive. If we need a sense of continuity most of the time, total continuity would kill us. Just as lobsters and snakes must slough their outer coverings periodically or be crushed by what protects them, so we must cast off our realities from time to time or die. To resist change too long is fatal, as much for organizations as for people. The eighteenth-century English thinker Edmund Burke, a traditionalist if there ever was one, put the problem well when he said, "A state without the means of some change is without the means of its conservation."

Thus we return to the issue of organizational change and the transition it causes by a route that makes it clearer why change is so disorienting. Transition is nothing less than the death and rebirth of a person's world. Personal worlds cannot change without disintegrating first. Remodeling provides a good analogy: There has to be destruction before there can be rebuilding; there is always a longer-than-promised time of confusion and mess; and it seems always to cost twice as much as they estimated that it would. These are not just the realities of the construction business but the laws of the universe, for everywhere the old form has to collapse into chaos before the new form can take shape. The individual's world and the organizations can only rise from the ashes of their own destruction.

It is ironic that it is so hard to remember these things, for we all know them in our bones. We have lived through dozens of significant transitions in our lives, although many of us mistakenly write these experiences off as irrelevant to organizational affairs on the grounds that they are "only personal."

Our cultural heritage also encourages us to disregard transition. Unlike more traditional societies that have developed sophisticated mourning rituals and regular ceremonies marking the ends of cycles, our society has emphasized new beginnings and has not believed that endings had any necessary significance. Without a sense of their significance, we hurry through them, denying our pain and trying to escape from it into a new beginning that somehow keeps vanishing whenever we draw near to it. Recent research on the terminally ill and the bereaved, however, has challenged this view of endings and the best way to deal with them. This research has organizational implications that we will note in the next chapter.

Our culture has also viewed empty time and space as essentially meaningless too, so it has been slow to appreciate the need for the neutral zone. Other cultures believe such emptiness to be a fertile time, a place of gestation. The Japanese, for example, speak of it not as empty but as "full of nothing" and regard it as the pregnant pause before beginning something new and different. While we are likely to view pauses as delays in a plan that ought to be proceeding with all possible speed, they view them as times of waiting for the right moment to act. They think of "right action" as a question of timing, while we think of it as a question of technique.*

Our technique-mindedness undercuts our sensitivity to transition even further by encouraging us to think of organizational change in a narrowly technical or financial sense. In the name of good business practices, we make decisions but forget that human beings have to carry them out. In spite of all the talk about people being an organization's primary resource, we keep making plans that assume that people are expendable.

Our awareness of transition is further blunted by the need to "sell" the changes that we propose to top management in a competitive atmosphere. Given the political realities of organizational life, it is tremendously tempting for the proponents of a plan to promise more than they can deliver. To be successful in the planning marketplace, one often feels compelled to claim that a proposed change will (1) solve the organization's problem completely, (2) not take very long or cost very much, and (3) not disrupt present operations significantly.

In fact, transition-generating changes are slow, expensive, and difficult. In *Corporate Cultures,* Deal and Kennedy estimate that an organizational change will take from 5 to 10 percent of the time and energy of the people it affects. My own work suggests that theirs is a very conservative estimate, based on changes that do not threaten anyone's world very seriously. When the change is deeper or more far-reaching, the percentage of effort and time taken up by the change can quickly rise to fifty or more. Yet even at 10 percent, the cost can be immense.

Given our cultural biases, our technical orientation, and our political temptations to oversell, it is not surprising that we have not developed much transition awareness in our organizations. But reasons are not justifications, especially when change is so constantly undermining the effectiveness of our organizations as it is today. What we need are ways to foresee and monitor the effects of transition and ways to manage its three phases. For at bottom, people's resistance to change is really difficulty with letting go of who they were, or difficulty with the ambiguities and emptiness of the neutral zone, or difficulty with the challenge of beginning anew. It is to each of those difficulties and to ways of dealing with them that we will turn in the next section of this book.

PART TWO

*MANAGING
THE
TRANSITION
PROCESS*

3: The End of the World

> Any real change implies the breakup of the world as one has always known it, the loss of all that gave one identity.
>
> James Baldwin, *Nobody Knows My Name*

Once one understands the dynamics of transition, one begins to see the need for endings everywhere. Every change in leadership terminates relationships and plans that had been central to people's worlds. Every merger takes away power and status that people had built their worlds upon. Every change in product lines or services brings to an end the functions and competencies that made people feel valuable and the groupings that made them feel at home. Even promotions require endings by causing people to leave behind their big-fish/little-pond worlds.

Every change, in short, causes losses. It doesn't matter if the change is large or small. As long as it breaks the old pattern, it will cause someone to lose something. (In *The Ordeal of Change* long-shoreman-philosopher Eric Hoffer recalled his days as a migrant picker when he left the pea fields of central California for the bean fields farther north: "I still remember how hesitant I was that first morning as I was about to address myself to the string bean vines," he wrote. "Would I be able to pick beans? Even the change from peas to string beans had in it elements of fear.")

The sense of loss is present even when the change is obviously for the better. One would imagine, for example, that winning a prestigious prize is such a positive change that one would forget any minor inconveniences that it might entail. But a number of Nobel Prize winners have told how the award brought to an end the time and conditions necessary for the kind of research or service or creative activity that had always made their lives meaningful.* On a more modest scale, promotions often entail losses of contact with the work or the peers that made one feel effective and comfortable. It is common to hear people lament the day they left the technical or creative roles that attracted them to the organization and moved up into management.

Studies of the relation between change and illness tell the same story. In their pioneering study of the impact of "life-change events," Thomas Holmes and Richard Rahe found that the effects on people of small changes were different only in degree, not in kind, from big ones. They found that planned changes were almost as disruptive as unplanned changes, and that positive changes, like a much desired marital reconciliation, the long awaited birth of a child, or a financial bonanza were only a little less difficult to assimilate than were negative changes.*

Organizational histories are likewise full of instances where positive changes entailed significant losses. The influx of money from an initial public offering of stock destroys the old organizational world at the same time that it creates the possibility of a new one. In a West Coast biotechnical company that I studied, the founder had run the organization with the informal systems he had used in his personal life. Financial records were no more than the checkbook for the corporate checking account. Budgeting was a month-by-month affair that depended on the current checkbook balance. Employment policies were whatever he worked out with particular individuals. Everyone loved the informality of the system. It is not surprising that they spoke of the influx of $15 million of new capital, the establishment of board of directors, the appearance of a financial officer and his formalized procedures as "the end of everything that made this a good place to work."

This sense of loss is usually especially confusing when it results from something that everyone has been working for. I belonged for eleven years to an association of families who built a jointly owned community of homes. We were dismayed to discover that when we had completed our difficult building project, which we had always viewed as merely the first chapter of our lives together, we had lost much of the joint purpose that had held us together. We had considered house building an obstacle to our real endeavor, but we found that once that "obstacle" was past, we began to experience more and more conflict and, as a result, several of the founders left.

It is particularly important to understand the change-transition-ending-loss connection in situations where the way in which you propose to deal with a change requires a still further change in people's behavior and in how they see themselves. For example, one of the truisms of humane management is that people will accept a change more readily if they are involved in planning it. That is true, but participating in planning can itself involve a significant loss. Peter Marris notes this paradox in describing what happened when people scheduled to be displaced in a London slum clearance project were included in the planning group: When people formerly without influence were invited to participate in decisions, they lost their irresponsibility. All their familiar attitudes to authority were invalidated. They were now the colleagues of administrators, not merely the clients of their services. They could no longer regard established power as beyond their control, a given factor of their circumstances. They sacrificed the old freedom of apathy or dissent for an influence whose rewards were unpredictable.*

As the epigraph of this chapter notes, it is their "identity" that people lose when things change significantly. In his study, "The Breakup of the Bell System," W. Brooke Tunstall sums up the findings of an immense survey of the reactions to the court-ordered breakup of American Telephone and Telegraph this way:

> Immediately after the divestiture experience there was a kind of identity crisis for AT&T people. A soft, collective voice almost could be heard saying: "I knew the old Bell System, its mission, its operation, its people, its culture. And I knew my niche in it. In that knowledge, I had identity and confidence about my company and myself. Now I work for a new company, one fourth its former size, with only a partial history and no track record. With the loss of our mission—universal service—and the fragmentation of the very business of providing telephone service, I find myself asking, 'Who are we?' 'Who am I?' "*

It is surprisingly difficult for people who are planning a change, convinced as they are likely to be of its value or at least its necessity to the organization, to see how it could be experienced as a loss. In my Organization Transition Seminars, we usually spend a long time on this issue, and I have found it useful to use a kind of checklist to help managers to see a change through the eyes of those it most affects. Losses characteristically fall into the following six categories:

Loss of Attachments
Loss of Turf
Loss of Structure
Loss of a Future
Loss of Meaning
Loss of Control

Transition always threatens our *attachments*—not only specific relationships and group memberships, but also our feeling "connected" in a larger sense.* Organizational changes disrupt both peer relationships and hierarchical ones. A new department, for example, may be carved out of several existing departments. Most of its new personnel are in some degree uprooted. Their former co-workers are gone—as is their boss, whose priorities were well-known, and their subordinates, who understood what was expected of them. Gone, too, is the collective "us" that provided a home base for their efforts. No matter how much sense the change makes and regardless of whether or not it looks personally advantageous, everyone assigned to the new department has been to some degree "orphaned" in the process.

People vary in how difficult they find this loss of attachment. (It may be true that, as John Donne said, "No man is an island," but it is also true that some people are connected to the mainland only during very, very low tides.) People whose "identity" is established mainly by roles and statuses and competencies always have an easier time ending attachments than others do. At the same time, they pay for their gain with a kind of loneliness that no amount of interpersonal contact can remove.

In contrast, there are many people whose identity is largely based on their relationships, and these people are always particularly vulnerable to the loss of *attachment.* This loss may, in fact, prove so painful that they simply cannot go through it; or they go through it but do not attach themselves to the new situation firmly for fear of experiencing another traumatic loss later.

One of the ways to help people deal with the loss of attachment is by using ritual. I am not necessarily thinking of formal or self-consciously ceremonial events, but rather of simple ways of recognizing publicly and tangibly the kinds of losses that are too often left unarticulated and private. I am thinking of something as simple as the warehouse foreman at a manufacturing plant where I was conducting a seminar who took two dozen workers out for pizza and beer and a Mets game on the night that the warehouse was shut down. He had no sense that he was being "ceremonial," but he delivered a little speech in which he said that they wouldn't be working together any more and that he was sorry because they were a hell of a bunch of guys. Several of the warehousemen made extemporaneous and emotional replies to what the foreman had said. It was, as one of them said later, "some evening!" and one that provided a sense of closure to a difficult situation.

Sometimes a more formal event can be very effective. When General Electric's Cuyahoga (Ohio) lamp plant was shut down, there was a big party on the final day of work. Here is how the party was described by one of the people who coordinated its logistics:

> During the last week of plant operations, graffiti paper was hung in each work group with the hope that feelings would be written. The walls soon became filled . . . with farewell statements. Interestingly, very few negative statements were made. The last day of production, the [coordinating committee] collected the graffiti and rehung it in the food-laden, balloon-filled cafeteria. Two hundred people still working in the plant on this day assembled on the third floor for a parade . . . Spontaneously the group began to sing "Old McDonald Had a Farm," with words inserted about life lived in the plant. "Farewell to Cuyahoga Party" began with much eating, music, and some dancing. The shift bell sounded and the plant manager began the "ritual" which closed the plant. Individuals made farewell statements, and the Vice President of Manufacturing spoke briefly, as did the Plant Manager. A large product display balloon was deflated to symbolize the closing of the plant and the assembled sang "God Bless America." The plant was closed. A large banner was hung announcing "THE BEGINNING OF SOMETHING NEW" for employees to see as they left.*

People let go of the past more easily and completely with the help of ritual, and that ease is translatable into better community relations and better morale among workers who may be reemployed elsewhere in the organization.

The second loss that may be experienced as part of the change-caused ending is the loss of *turf.* I use this term broadly to refer to everything from people's physical territories to fields of responsibility based on their expertise. Songbirds define their turf vocally, wolves urinate on the perimeter of theirs, little fish called sticklebacks patrol invisible lines down the center of their aquariums— and we define our turf by a thousand subtle and tacit agreements to treat an actual or a symbolic "area" as though it belonged to us.

Questions of precedent are always referred to Susan, while tasks involving computers go to Sam; a decision regarding marketability can't be made without Stuart's input, and if something affects the image of the organization in the eyes of the public, everyone knows that Sandra had better be consulted. These conventions develop partly because of actual skill and experience, but also because of a subtle kind of division of labor, the goal of which is to give everyone a place and predictable way of participating in the joint effort.

The introduction of new technology usually leads to the loss of turf or the threat of such loss, for the way in which turf was distributed under one technology is seldom directly convertible into what is appropriate to the new one. The items in question may be the metal axes that Westerners introduced into a Polynesian culture— axes that led to a deadly power struggle between the totem group that claimed stone axes as their domain and the totem group that claimed metal objects as theirs. Or it may be a computer, which the younger workers like to use and their elders won't touch.

Sometimes technology threatens employees' worlds in unexpected ways, as when putting computers on executives' desks in one company gave them direct access to performance data which previously had reached them only indirectly, through their subordinates. They viewed the change as a significant gain, but the subordinates did not, for they had lost the time they had once had to correct problems before their superiors knew about them. In the end, the data-access programs had to be rewritten to make data inaccessible for a day or two to anyone but the person directly responsible for the situation it described.*

Any change that involves how or where things are done in an organization is likely to lead to losses of turf, especially since the location and size of one's working area are an important aspect of one's turf. One need only to suggest remodeling an office layout to discover that human beings are as territorial as larks or gorillas. (It is suggestive that a recent survey by a relocation consulting firm showed that 68 percent of the office managers who were in charge of company relocations were either fired or demoted after the move.* Whenever there is scapegoating of that kind, you can be sure that a painful and badly managed ending has occurred in the organization.)

There is scarcely an area of organizational change where managers show less sensitivity and where a little sensitivity would pay bigger dividends than in dealing with losses of turf. The secret here is imagining how the change looks from the other person's point of view. How has change invaded the person's psychological space? How has it cost the person some professional territory? Nothing can be done until one knows these things.

Because one's own reactions have a way of getting displaced onto others, it is important to let people report their own experience directly. Questions must be asked sympathetically, of course. I remember one manufacturing manager who reported that he had had a good talk with his supervisors and now understood their point of view, although later I learned that he had opened the meeting with the question, "What's this horseshit I hear about your being unhappy with your new duties?"

Beyond empathetic communication, the basic turf-management technique is negotiation.* The heart of negotiation is discovering and discussing *interests,* rather than presenting and trying to balance fixed *positions.* When someone says that you can't give the task to Harry because it's Bob's responsibility, he is taking a position. You can take the opposite position, and the fight will be on. Or you can determine his interest—which may be in protecting Bob's turf, but may also be in protecting his own (which he may wrongly believe to be also in question). Or it may actually be in protecting the union's right to have a voice in settling turf issues, or it may be in getting the work to be done in the hands of those best qualified to do it. These interests would be served by quite different solutions, and your own interest in getting the work done expeditiously could be similarly taken care of in several ways. You can negotiate solutions that recognize and serve everyone's legitimate but very different interests, but mutually exclusive positions cannot be maintained intact, and someone is going to have to sacrifice more turf to make them fit.

The third thing that is likely to be experienced as a loss in an ending is *structure*. The details of the change do not matter: They may be physical or interpersonal or functional or procedural. But whatever they are, the resulting loss of structure makes people feel as though their worlds have just come apart and they have been left exposed to a world that is empty and chaotic. In a profile of Walter Bauer, who had been ousted as the CEO of Informatics General Corp. after that California software company had been taken over by a bigger company, the interviewer notes that the biggest problem Bauer faced was "the shift from a fast-paced 10- or 12-hour day to the unsettling quiet of one's own home."*

The issue is not that organizations have a "structure" that can be pictured in a wall chart. The structure I am talking about is more psychological than physical. Whatever their other and more practical justifications, all the patterns of authority, policies, schedules, deadlines, and physical arrangements of an organizational situation are ways of protecting people from the chaos of a life without structure. People who lose this kind of structuring suddenly are like deep-sea divers who depressurize too quickly. If they depended a great deal on the external structure of their lives for a sense of who they are, such people will be completely incapacitated by the psychological "bends" when they lose that structure.

If you are not such a person, you may not readily recognize the structure-loss potential of a situation. In such a case, you are likely to find the person who is structure-sensitive "unreasonably upset" about a change. You will probably try to explain the details of and the reason for the change accurately—as though once the person "understands," the reaction will be more "normal." You will be perplexed by the person's depth of feeling about something that "isn't really that big a deal." You need to recognize that the change leads to the loss of the way the person had of making his or her life feel in order and under control. It is no wonder that the person makes a big deal out of it.

In the next chapter we will discuss in more detail the problem of dealing with structurelessness, for the neutral zone is by nature a place and a time without structure. At this point let us simply note that as old schedules and policies and spatial arrangements disappear, new temporary ones need to be developed. The emphasis here is on "temporary," for it is unwise to commit yourself to a complete set of new permanent arrangements until you have had a chance to live with the new situation for a while. That does not mean, however, that interim patterns cannot be established. (The fired CEO referred to above, for example, found that setting himself a regular nine-to-five schedule during his search for a new position was very important, as was setting up a small but complete "office" at home.)

Because it is difficult for people in an organization to recall the details of short-term agreements and arrangements, it is important that everyone know how to check on what they are. Organizations in change often do well to set up a Transition Hot Line staffed by people who have current information about how or when something is to be done during the transition. Western Airlines did this after the announcement of its acquisition by Delta, and the results were excellent.

The fourth loss that a person may experience when impacted by organizational change is the loss of a *future*. Although we are unlikely to be aware of it until it isn't there anymore, all of us carry around an expected future in our heads and hearts. In fact, for many people the present is acceptable or unacceptable largely in terms of the future it is believed to lead to. Any organization that changes its retirement policies or its pension benefits is sure to discover quickly how important it is to people to know that a particular future lies ahead of them.

The connection may not be so obvious with other kinds of changes, where the future is undermined more indirectly. In a large aerospace company where I consulted, plans for a major reorganization generated a great deal of anxiety and unhappiness among the engineers. The plans involved the reassignment of most engineers from a single central department to one of six new business units, each devoted to the development and manufacture of a particular type of aerospace product. The aspect of this change that most distressed the engineers was that their career paths no longer led up through a professional hierarchy where they were evaluated by colleagues with similar technical expertise. Henceforth, their promotability would be judged by "business" people who were product-

and customer-oriented, people who (in the words of one worried engineer) "wouldn't know a thermo-couple if it pissed on his foot." Under these circumstances, every engineer faced a completely unknown future.

People vary considerably in how important the future is to them. Some of us have to know just where we are headed, while others of us are comfortable being lilies of the field with no thought for the morrow. Some of us are dreamers, who can generate a new future in a minute, and others are planners, whose future takes months to heal from relatively small wounds.

Whatever our personal style, the loss of a future is most disturbing if it forces us to recognize that we will probably not realize our dreams. It is much more difficult to let go of a dream of getting to the top of the organizational pyramid, making some big professional contribution, or accumulating a lot of money than it is simply to lose a chance for a particular promotion. When a dream is the casualty, the result can be out of all relation to the demonstrable effects of the change itself, for then the change becomes a vehicle for a much deeper transition: letting go of the dreams that motivated our efforts up to that point.

Once the loss of a future is recognized as a problem, relatively minor revisions in the planned changes can sometimes solve it. But where future-loss is unavoidable, it is wise to give the affected people the resources and information needed to replan their futures. Laid-off employees are often given job-hunting assistance, but retained employees may need career-development help just as much if the organizational changes have blocked the paths they had planned to follow. After the recent work-force reductions and the resulting reorganization at Exxon, an employee commented, "So many managers have been demoted, there is a layer on top of me—people in their 40s and 50s—that I'll never get through. For the survivors, there are no opportunities. Moving up is a thing of the past."* Unable to see any way around the roadblock, the speaker was looking for a job elsewhere.

Some organizations take a very antagonistic attitude toward such people and would be likely to reject what is really the best way to deal with them, namely, to give them career-planning and, if necessary, job-hunting assistance. They fear that career-building assistance will be used as "outplacement" assistance for people that the organization does not want to lose. But organizations that have tried it have found that such help more often than not is used within the organization as a kind of "*in*placement" and that it does several very positive things.

First, it breaks down the feeling of hopelessness that undermines morale and feeds hostility. An employee who feels trapped is much more dangerous than an employee who feels that he could leave if he wanted to. Second, it allies the organization and the employee against a common problem, which is that change has messed up everyone's plans. Nothing rebuilds loyalty faster than a practical demonstration of mutual interest.

Finally, if it is properly designed, such career-development assistance does not focus on finding a job with someone else but on finding the opportunities inside the organization that correspond to the employees' abilities, interests, and temperaments. I have found such seminars very effective in my work with the U.S. Forest Service, whose work force has been cut sharply and whose responsibilities have been redefined because of budget reductions and a drop in the cutting of timber. In many cases, employees have used the assistance to find new positions for themselves in parts of the Forest Service where more people were needed. In other cases, employees have left the Forest Service for the chance to set up business on their own—only to return and do parts of their old jobs for the Forest Service more inexpensively as independent contractors than as employees.

Life planning of a general sort—including financial planning, health planning, and legal advice as well as career development per se—is a very valuable benefit to offer employees whose assumptions and dreams have been disrupted by change.

Such life-planning assistance must be process-, not product-, oriented. That is, any particular plan can provide only short-term assistance to an employee. Employees need a way to continue to respond positively and creatively to the changes that an increasingly turbulent world guarantees they will face in the future. It is useful to take some of the focus off the particular change of the moment and shift it to the issue of change itself. (See chapter 9, "Making

Change Work for You," for a description of what such a program needs to cover.)

A fifth loss likely to be experienced as a result of organizational changes is the loss of *meaning*. To some extent meaning is always at risk in an ending, though this is so in different ways for different people. For some people, life loses its meaning when attachments are broken. For others, meaning is lost when turf disappears. For others it is the loss of structure or the loss of the future that makes life suddenly seem meaningless. Whatever the specifics, change threatens meaning in everyone's life.

The clue to the presence of this loss is attempting to counter it by wrestling persistently with the question Why? This struggle to recover meaning may involve specific questions or it may simply involve the repeated statement, "I don't understand. I just don't understand." It may involve rational theorizing or wild suspicions, blame or self-blame. But whatever form it takes, it reminds us how crucial to a person's identity and well-being it is for things to make sense and not to be pointless or crazy. It is sometimes even preferable to hold on to the irrational idea that one has caused all the trouble oneself than to believe that everything is meaningless.

When the meaningfulness of an organizational situation breaks down, a reality vacuum develops and all kinds of "meanings" rush in to fill it. Rumors abound: "You know the real reason the V.P. left?" "The CEO's secretary says they're getting ready to do all our manufacturing over in Korea." "The board had given the president three months to get back into the black, I heard . . ." In this situation, there is a kind of psychological turbulence, as different and conflicting meanings collide. It is particularly important, at such a time, for the organization's leaders to establish their view of why everything is happening. Needless to say, it needs to be a factually based view—anything else just sets the stage for a later round of disillusionment. But within that limitation, there is room for different realities, and one of the leader's main tasks is to get his or her reality across to the organization's personnel.

Communication is usually conceived of as the transmission of information, but it is also the expression of meaning. Many organizational communication systems are quite inadequate to that task, and so times of organizational change are by definition times of communications redesign. Memos are a terrible medium for expressing meaning, though most organizations use them as though they were meant for that purpose. Because meaning is personal, public presentations by leaders, as well as video or audio tapes of such presentations, are far better. Personal letters are also useful.

But care needs to be taken that the official meaning not be so mechanically applied that it crushes individual attempts to make sense out of the situation. In a study called "Adjustment to Threatening Events," UCLA psychologist Shelley Taylor shows how people come to terms with traumatic experiences by endowing them with personal meaning.* To insist that they see events impersonally is to destroy that meaning.

This leaves the manager in a paradox: He must honor the individual's picture of what is happening, but he must also assert what he believes to be the "real" reason. This is certainly difficult, but good managers instinctively do it. At the very least, the manager must understand that he can easily win the argument about why something happened, but lose the war of getting people to go along with it.

A particularly painful kind of meaning loss occurs when one's organization or its leadership is accused of doing something wrong. We all want to believe in our co-workers, our superiors, the CEO, and the organization itself. Our identity overlaps with those other identities, and if those others or the organization itself prove to be false in some significant way, the results can be devastating.

After the publicity given to the E. F. Hutton check-kiting scheme, employees kept up a good public front but talked about little else with one another. A reporter who interviewed employees at that time reported a number of indications of the loss of faith they felt—little things, like the man who stopped wearing his company T-shirt when jogging. At Johns Manville Corporation, the senior vice-president for human resources reflected long after the initial impact of the asbestos cases, "It is still tough when you're sitting in the backyard at a Saturday afternoon barbecue and somebody gets to talking about the asbestos situation." And during the OPEC price rise of the early seventies, some Sun Oil employees reacted to public criticism of oil company profits by pretending at cocktail parties that they worked for the company's ship-building subsidiary rather than for the oil company itself. Robert Watts, the executive vice-president of A. H. Robins, which is currently facing more than 300,000 claims for harm from using its Dalkon Shield contraceptives has said that he "sits in the back pew at church on Sundays and leaves as soon as the service ends."*

The loss of faith is not always tied to a specific situation or event this way. It is sometimes the result of a slow change in the public image of the organization. Many U.S. Forest Service employees, for example, began to work for that agency at a time when it was widely praised as the protector of wilderness and the natural environment. But a decade of criticism of the Forest Service's cooperation with the timber industry has changed that, and now the agency is the target of frequent and sometimes violent protest.

During a training session that I conducted with the staff of a large national forest, the forest supervisor was called from the room for half an hour. He came up and apologized at our next break, explaining that he had been called out to deal with the problem of a man who had chained himself to the top of a 150-foot Douglas fir tree that was scheduled to be felled for a road. "This isn't the same organization I joined," he said sadly. "You'd think we were the powers of evil. Why, tomorrow we have a meeting to decide how to deal with the spikes that groups like Earth First! are telling activists to drive into trees—spikes that'll explode the sawmill saws when they're cut into. I hear they're even using ceramic spikes that won't show up on metal detectors. I get angry with that kind of crazy behavior, but then I get angry too at the Forest Service for getting itself—and for getting me—in the middle of bitterness I never asked for."

Whether you are the power company employee who used to be the good guy who brought electricity to our houses but are now the bad guy who threatens everyone with PCB-filled transformers and nuclear power plants, or the executive of Union Carbide trying to assert your company's concern for human life in the face of the Bhopal, India, disaster. Whether you are a junior appointee in the Nixon administration as the reality of the Watergate fiasco unfolds and the boss doggedly denies any wrongdoing, or the NASA employee who sees your organization transformed overnight from the home of the Right Stuff to the scene of confusion, distrust, and shame after the Challenger explosion in early 1986—whatever the circumstances, the fact that you were drawn to an organization because you believed in it means that you will lose part of yourself when you lose faith in the organization.

There is no way out of the faith-threatening situation except honesty about responsibility and a regrouping to go forward on a positive note. The facts must be faced. Disillusionments need to be discussed openly within the organization. Top company officials must be publicly visible and to speak forthrightly. Fact-finding groups should go into action and announce their findings quickly. If disciplinary actions are appropriate, they must be fair and decisive.

And then there should be a team-building effort to pull everyone together. After the recall of millions of bottles of potentially poisoned Tylenol, Johnson & Johnson employees sprouted WE'RE COMING BACK buttons. After a couple of crashes that happened one after another for unrelated reasons, McDonnell Douglas employees put I'M PROUD OF THE DC-10 bumper stickers on their cars. To outsiders, these things may seem silly or even defensive. But if they are not done to cover up the facts, they can be important aids in weathering the transition.

Whenever meaning and faith are undermined, the biblical figure of Job is the image of us all. He was brought down to ruin, not simply by the physical losses he suffered, but even more by his inability to understand why God would make him suffer that way. That inability to understand is repeated in every change that undermines the way employees find meaning in work. You see it in the puzzled look. You hear it in the frightened voice: "It doesn't make sense. Nothing makes sense. It's crazy. Why did they do it? Who made this decision?" It is Job in a business suit.

The example of Job reminds us that those questions are hard to answer and that answers (such as they are) may not do as much good as we comforters wish that they did. After his three "comforters" had had their say, Job burst out: "How long will ye vex my soul, and break me to pieces with words?" What Job is saying is that his questions are not meant to elicit information but are part of a larger struggle to come to terms with change-induced losses. What Job is doing is what all of us do when we come to an important ending in our lives—he is mourning or grieving.

Anyone concerned with keeping the transition process from disrupting organizational effectiveness needs to understand grieving, because, as Peter Marris has written, "The management of change depends upon our ability to articulate the process of grieving . . . When loss cannot be articulated, its suppressed tensions will in the end prove more profoundly disruptive than the social conflicts which relieve them."*

This is a hard lesson for supervisors or co-workers to learn, because the anger and sadness, the despair and disorientation that are essential to grieving are difficult to witness, especially when the witness is either at least partly responsible for the decision that is producing the distress or also needs to grieve but is denying that need. Either situation is likely to lead to distorted and unhelpful responses—to punitive action or demands that the mourners be "rational," or think positively, or stop feeling sorry for themselves.

Whenever I go into an organization where a large layoff is in the works, where a familiar product line is being discontinued, or where technology is rendering old ways obsolete, I am sure to hear that morale is down. The speaker is likely to be looking for ways to bring it back up. I can certainly sympathize with that wish, but as a starting point for useful action it is as inappropriate as is the wish that a widow or widower would stop grieving. In each case the supposed problem is not something that can be made to go away; rather it is a part of a process that needs to be facilitated.

Everything that is known about loss makes it clear that to make some part of grieving go away simply aborts natural healing and leads to long-term trouble. Transition management, therefore, must begin with finding ways to legitimate grieving so that losses are worked through to acceptance.

The first thing that such legitimation usually requires is an educational effort. Leaders need to understand grieving and show through their words and deeds that it is acceptable within the organization. Managers and supervisors must learn to distinguish the symptoms of grieving from those that simply demonstrate a poor attitude or low motivation. And the employees themselves can profit from learning about grieving, just as bereaved people can, because without such information it is easy for them to feel that they are not coping well or are actually showing signs of psychological illness.

People who have studied grieving agree on three things: First, it takes a surprisingly long time—months, certainly, and even years—to work through; second, it has several phases, and each is characterized by different patterns of feeling and thinking; and third, it naturally leads to the expression of emotions that are uncomfortable for most of us, either in ourselves or in others.

In his classic study called simply *Loss,* the English psychiatrist John Bowlby says that there are essentially four phases to mourning:*

1. A phase of numbing that usually lasts from a few hours to a week and may be interrupted by outbursts of extremely intense distress and/or anger.

2. A phase of yearning and searching for [whatever has been lost] lasting some months and sometimes for years.

3. A phase of disorganization and despair.

4. And a phase of greater or less degree of reorganization.

The third phase belongs to the neutral zone and will be discussed at length in the next chapter, while the fourth phase belongs to the new beginning, which is the subject of chapter 5. It is the first two phases that we will discuss here, for they constitute the ending proper.

The phase of numbness is the result of our natural self-protective resistance to experiences or information that violate our reality. It is a form of *denial,* a way of saying "It can't be so." In the first hours or days after something has ended, denial maintains hope and protects the person from total demoralization. If it lasts beyond that time, however, denial causes trouble because it keeps the person from moving on into the rest of the grieving process.

In an organizational setting, denial can take many forms:

"They're just trying to scare us. They'd never really do that."

"They're always making these announcements. Just wait and it'll blow over."

"What did they say they were going to do with the excess people? I can't remember."

"I'm not going to worry. Everything always turns out for the best."

[In the middle of a tense meeting announcing forthcoming changes] "Hey, didja hear the one about the two lawyers . . ."

Many managers like the denial phase, because at that time they seldom have to deal with the actual pain caused by an ending. Because it is comfortable in that way, they may unconsciously collaborate to keep it going. They may withold information that would make the change more real, or they may agree with the rationalizations used by the people to keep from facing the new reality. But because denial insulates people from the reality of what is going on and delays the process of coming to terms with that reality, the wise manager will make the basic facts known from the start and continue to paint a realistic picture as time goes on.

As Bowlby says, the phase of numbing may be punctuated by moments of anger. This is not an emotion that many organizational people see as functional to the conduct of business, but during grieving it is quite important. The anger—which may be completely misdirected, especially at first—is a good sign, for it shows that the person's system of active self-defense is beginning to take over. For this reason, it is important that people on whom the anger is displaced have some idea of its source; otherwise they will take it personally and try to cut it off.

The second phase of grieving is characterized by Bowlby as a time of "yearning and searching." This is a time of mood swings between hope and discouragement, between attempts to hold on to what is threatened and attempts to face its loss. It is likely to be a time of what Elisabeth Kübler-Ross has termed *bargaining*—the attempt (overt or covert) to strike a deal by which the loss is forestalled or minimized.* In its overt form, employees may take the manager aside and suggest that they can do something special to help or that they are willing to take on some new assignment or that they have the answer to the manager's dilemma. More covertly, the bargaining may take the form of excessive cooperativeness or other placating behavior. And it may be completely covert, in the form of secret bargains struck with God: "Get me out of this situation with my skin intact, and I promise that I'll . . ." (In *Hannah and Her*

Sisters, Woody Allen offers a memorable portrayal of bargaining in his monologue aimed at God, as he waits in the hospital for the results of his CAT scan.)

More functional than the bargaining, which always has a slightly unreal quality about it, may be practical activity meant to determine whether there really are alternatives to the loss. Employees may go and talk to the department head to see whether she has considered another possibility. Employees may begin to collect signatures on a petition or do other things to organize support for their cause. They may start studying the issues facing the organization, reading books and attending classes.

Yet, even as they do this, they are likely to be swept by great waves of discouragement and sadness. Most managers find sadness hard to deal with and fall into the trap of trying to make it go away. They try to point out the good side of the change; they try to dull the edge of pain by pretending that things may not be as final as they seem; and they may finally fall back on blaming the one who is grieving: "It really makes me mad to see you moping around like this! Now get off your ass and get back to work! You know you'll feel better tomorrow."

Trying to make sadness go away doesn't do much good, and blaming people for it does real harm. Such reactions only drive the behavior out of sight, where it is more disruptive than it is out in the open; and they block the natural progress of grieving by making the person divert energy into controlling it. Much more helpful is an acceptance of emotional response as legitimate, but a clear limit on acting it out in destructive ways. ("It's OK to yell, but I don't want to see you hit the machine with that wrench again!") And you should encourage talk. Expressing the natural anger and sadness, recollecting the importance of what is being lost, and fears for the future without it all help the person to come to terms with the loss.

All of the research on loss agrees that openly expressed reaction to loss is the best possible avenue for working it through and letting go of the bygone situation and the identity one had in it. A failure to work the loss through looks from the outside as though there were no loss, but it is likely to turn out later that the person is still holding on to the past in ways that leave little energy for the future.

A final loss is the loss of *control.* Many changes result from situations that we have no control over. Even top executives often feel powerless to affect the outcome of the changes that are transforming their organizations. It is not just that they have no choices, for they often have to make difficult choices that will affect many people. It is that there is no way to know what the right choice is—and, worse, that there is no choice that will not cause some people deep pain.

I recently watched a group of middle managers being told about a change to a new, "flatter" organization, with less space and more communication between the top and the bottom. (It is one of those changes that we consultants sometimes urge on our clients without warning them of the wrenching transitions that will be necessary to make it happen.) These particular managers were going to have to be bumped up and down and sideways to make the reorganization work, for they then occupied the four levels in the organizational chart that were being compressed into two levels. Some of them were actually going to benefit from the changes, and none of them was going to be penalized financially as a result of them. But none of them had chosen the changes and none of them could know in the long run what their outcome would be.

All the talk about improved communication and clearer responsibilities fell on deaf ears, for all that they could hear was that the decision had already been made, and made without their needs being considered. It was out of their control. Within a week, the first signs of resistance to the change had begun to show up in the form of communication problems and a general sagging of productivity.

As with all of the other losses, the loss of control hits some people harder than others. Those most at risk are the people whose well-being is dependent on being in control at all times—the people who have their days planned down to the minute, who have everything in labeled boxes in the storeroom, and who insist on knowing exactly what everybody is going to bring to the Christmas party. These people are only more exaggerated versions of us all, however, for everyone is uncomfortable with a life where everything is up for grabs and all their attempts to influence outcome count for nothing.

How does one deal with a feeling among employees that control has been lost in a change? While getting affected employees involved in the planning process is not a panacea, anything that gives people a feeling of regaining some control is a gain. Experiments with Stop buttons at each worker's place on an assembly line show that, after the first few days, they are not very often used; but they provide the feeling of being in control of something that *could* get out of control. The same thing happens when a surgery patient is told that he or she can take a whiff of anesthetic "if you need it." The point is that being in control is a subjective experience and needs to be nurtured.

The control must be real or else disillusionment is likely to set in. Care needs to be exercised that people are not led to believe that they can decide or influence the decision about something when in fact they cannot. If decisions have already been made at the home office, it is self-defeating to pretend that they can be made in the field. But the home office is going to create unnecessary problems for itself if it insists on making all the decisions. Choice can, at the very least, be built into the implementation phase of most changes, and that choice can be an important part of each individual's personalizing the change. It is wise to remember that there are very few goals that can be reached by only one standardized path and that there are very few roles that have to be filled in only one style.

Some organizational changes take place under circumstances that are so close to utter disaster that no one has time to be concerned with who is losing what. But far more often, the needs of the moment are used to cover the discomfort of allowing oneself to be aware of the pain that people always feel when their worlds come to an end in some significant way. Being aware of pain is itself a source of pain, and it is easy to justify inattention by saying that we don't need any more pain . . . not now . . . not when everything is in transition like this.

That attitude, though certainly understandable, is very short-sighted. As Terrence Deal has written: "We rarely recognize that changes in the nature of work also create losses that trigger powerful individual or collective reactions. The costs may not be immediately obvious nor reflected directly in tangible ways, but left unattended over time, pressure builds up and can become a silent killer in organizations—much like hypertension in the human body."*

The analogy to stress-related illnesses is not just a figure of speech. Studies of groups of people who have been affected by large and sudden changes show that many of them display a consistent set of physical symptoms. People who lost their homes or loved ones in the eruption of Mt. St. Helens, for example, experienced (in the words of one report) "depression, changes in appetite, sleeplessness, loss of energy and ability to concentrate; generalized anxiety and unexpected bursts of panic; physical tension, shakiness, heart pounding, lightheadedness, jitteryness, . . . dreams, numbing, [and] feeling isolated from the rest of the world."* Not every change is so traumatic, of course, but many employees who are sweating out a merger or a cutback or a reorganization develop these same kinds of symptoms.

In view of the personal losses suffered in the course of organizational transition, it is no wonder that people often comment that employees aren't quite *there.* No wonder that all the slick talk about how terrific the new situation will be goes right over the employees' heads. No wonder employees look for little ways to slow things down, to give themselves time, to hold on to pieces of the world they have known. No wonder they get sick or have accidents at rates double those of the days before they were in transition. No wonder they jump ship when the first safe harbor appears. No wonder they become distrustful and hard to manage. No wonder they practice ingeniously disastrous acts of sabotage—like the word-processing employee who reprogrammed his San Francisco company's payroll to self-destruct when his name was removed from it.

But these results are not automatic. They are largely the artifact of unforeseen and mismanaged endings—of losses that were not acknowledged and compensated for. The effective management of endings and the losses they entail is the first, most necessary, and most frequently overlooked step in managing an organizational transition. It is not only good human relations. It is also good business.

4: Taking Them Through the Wilderness

> . . . insight comes at a moment of transition . . . at a break
> in periods of voluntary effort . . .
>   Rollo May, *The Courage to Create**

> The crisis consists precisely in the fact that the old is dying and
> the new cannot be born; in this [gap between the two] a great
> variety of morbid symptoms appears.
>   Antonio Gramsci, *The Prison Notebooks**

The ending, which launches the transition process, is often its most painful phase. But the least understood and most perplexing part of transition is the next phase, the neutral zone. Our culture offers even less help with the neutral zone than it does with the ending that precedes it, for modern Western societies have largely forgotten the importance of this strange in-between time, this gap between an old reality and a new one. In many ancient times and distant places, people in transition spent this in-between time in the wilderness, and they returned from it transformed and renewed. We, on the other hand, rush through this time, and fail thereby either to relinquish the old completely or to find anything adequate to replace it. And without even realizing it, we are exposed there to great dangers.

Although the neutral zone is no longer widely recognized, everyone who has ever changed careers or been through a divorce or lost a loved one knows something about it. At such times, one feels disoriented and confused, hopeful one moment and despairing the next, a little crazy, very alone, and unable to communicate effectively with others. "Life" seems to be something that is taking place beyond an invisible glass partition. People out there go through their motions and move their mouths like people talking to one another. But their actions and their words are empty and meaningless.

When an organization is going through a significant change, this confused and empty feeling can pervade the corridors and offices and shops of every building. People go about their tasks mechanically, and an outsider might think that things were going smoothly. But they are not. People's minds and hearts are elsewhere. In spite of the fact that there is more to do than ever, the employees move like people in a dream or waste their days in endless bickering. People talk but do not communicate; they listen but they do not hear. The days pass with little getting done.

This archetypal gap between the old and new occurs, for example, when one company acquires another. Everyone in the acquired company knows that their old mores, their old patterns of authority, and their old structure of responsibilities have lost their legitimacy; yet replacements for them have not yet been established and internalized. Other situations when the interim between old and new gapes open in an equally dangerous way come when a department is split in two, when the leadership at a facility changes, and when the roles in an organization have to be redefined after a layoff.

In failing to recognize the neutral zone and failing to provide ways to deal with it effectively, our culture handicaps changing organizations in two equally dangerous ways. First, it fails to warn them of the perils in the strange gap between the old and the new, where practical systems of control break down. Critical decisions are often bungled during the changeover from one leader or one procedure to another. In between times are by nature times when people are exposed to new dangers, so it is no accident that 85 percent of all kidnappings and assassinations take place in transit between one location and another.*

Many of the organizational dangers in the neutral zone come from within rather than without. When the systems of control break down, so does the force holding the organizational façade in place. What is likely to emerge at such times is what Carl Jung called the *shadow*, that part of the total identity which is suppressed and denied in the name of "living up to our ideals." The organizational shadow is, thus, the mirror image to the official culture that everyone espouses, just as the individual shadow is the opposite of the person's public image. Examples of organizational shadows include the suppressed greediness behind the altruistic façade of nonprofit organizations, the suppressed disorganization behind the by-the-numbers façade of a technologically sophisticated company, the suppressed hostility behind a hospital's façade of loving care, the suppressed laziness and inactivity behind the façade of an aggressive financial institution. You can count on the emergence of some elements of the shadow in the neutral zone, and you can count on those in authority being shocked by them, while those nearer the bottom of the hierarchy whisper that they knew it all along.

These perils are complicated because individual systems of control also break down in the neutral zone. Individual shadows may become visible: Mr. Nice Guy explodes, Ms. Happy Face gets very depressed. Individuals feel as though they are falling apart. In the vacuum left, as the quote at the beginning of this chapter says, old and almost forgotten anxieties emerge like figures in a dream.

But, difficult as that is, it is only half of the difficulty that comes from our culture's failure to recognize the wilderness between old and new. The second consequence of that failure is that we lose our access to the positive side of the neutral zone. The vacuum that draws out the suppressed shadow and the forgotten fear is also an empty space in which something new and creative can take place. It is in that emptiness that one gains what Rollo May calls "insight," and what others might call a vision of the future. The terrifying and the creative are really only the two faces of the same neutral zone chaos, and in each case one is faced with what Kierkegaard called "the dizziness of possibility."

It is in the neutral zone that people and organizations have the opportunity to be most creative. In cultures that we wrongly consider more primitive than ours, people willingly (though fearfully) sought out that wilderness state and the creativity it unlocks on vigils and Vision Quests, on pilgrimages to sacred places and journeys into the desert. Even in our own culture, creative and reflective individuals still seek that fertile solitude in various ways. But in our organizations, we usually consider it a waste of valuable time.

The common failure to distinguish transition from change leaves us unprepared for this dizziness, for it treats transition in general and the neutral zone in particular as just the state of changing. We think of changing as being like crossing the street: Once you step off the curb of the old situation, you should get across to the new situation as fast as you can. You would be foolish to stay out in the traffic any longer than necessary, and the last thing you would do would be to sit down in the middle of the street and take stock of where you want to go or (heaven forbid) who you really are.

That is a fair enough model for change, for often only a decisive change can dislodge a long-standing situation. As David Lloyd George said, "The most dangerous thing in the world is to leap a chasm in two jumps." But the bigger the jump needed to cross the chasm, the bigger the resulting transitions are likely to be, and the more profound is likely to be the chaos of the neutral zone.

A plan for getting people through the neutral zone must have two aspects. First, there must be strategies for supporting people during this interim when the ordinary organizational and personal structuring systems do not work very well. Second, there must be strategies for giving people access to the innovativeness and the vision that are always present in the neutral zone. Without the support, the creativity may not be released because people are too anxious or defensive. And without the creativity, much of the real value of the transition will have been lost. The challenge of neutral zone management is how to provide an interim system of temporary policies, procedures, responsibilities, and authority structures to get people through the neutral zone intact, without blocking their access to the insights and the discoveries that the neutral zone contains.

The first aspect of neutral-zone management is based on an understanding of what happens when people lose the external routines and controls that channeled their efforts into effective operations and gave them a way of structuring their lives. To help people across this gap successfully, several neutral-zone management strategies have proved useful:

First, creating temporary procedures and policies to govern activities in the interim between the known past and the unknown future. These are like the "winter rules" in golf, that govern play under conditions that are too rough or unpredictable to play by the regular rules. These policies and procedures might govern expenditures during a time when the organizational structure no longer corresponded to the one for which the budget was written. They might deal with expectations of and responsibilities for quality control during a changeover from one technology to another. They might mean setting up new channels of communication that are required by the new, temporary needs to talk about new problems with new people. Whatever they involve, these temporary arrangements provide guidelines or channels for action that might otherwise come to a halt.

Second, creating temporary lines of authority and responsibility, shaped by the needs of the neutral zone. These temporary responsibilities and authorities often work best if they are clustered into a Transition Management Group that is charged with the responsibility for calling the shots during the neutral-zone phase of the transition—much as the captain of a ship may be in command of the troops on board during a crossing. The interim management group may in part duplicate the old, fixed roles, for some of the latter may still be necessary to keep existing operations going until the new ones can take over. But some of the other roles will be specific to transition—liaison roles, for example, between units that never used to communicate but suddenly need to.

Third, doing whatever is possible to encourage cohesion within the organization as a whole and within its component units during the period spent in the neutral zone. The anxiety that many people feel in the neutral zone, together with the natural self-protectiveness of people whose worlds are being undermined, cause groups to fragment into separate individuals. People get competitive when they see the familiar positions disappearing, and if the transition managers don't intervene, a mess can result. Properly managed, however, the neutral zone can be a place of enhanced solidarity among employees and a sense of belonging that is almost impossible to create at any other time. We often, in fact, look back at times of crisis as times when "we all pulled together."

Fourth, expecting old issues to surface and trying not to choke them off as irrelevant to the present situation. Any organization sweeps its unresolved conflicts and distresses under the rug of a collective reality, and every neutral zone lifts a corner of that rug. "You aren't going to bring up *that* old issue, are you?" asks a supervisor in frustration. Of course, the answer is "yes." The neutral zone brings everything out of the closet, and while that is frustrating when you are trying to get other things accomplished, it is also (and must be treated as) an opportunity to put some old and unresolved issues to rest.

Fifth, taking care to keep the reasons for the organizational ending in people's minds so that the anxieties and confusions of the neutral zone do not lead them to try to escape from the chaotic present back into the simpler past. That great neutral-zone leader Moses typifies the problem faced by the management of an organization in transition. After some months in the wilderness, Moses' followers began "to murmur," as the Old Testament put it. They said, in effect, "Egypt wasn't so bad, was it? Why did we ever leave there, anyway?" He had to remind them how untenable their position there had become and how unrealistic their simplistic picture of the past was. He recognized that getting people through the wilderness of the neutral zone required not only a clear view of the opportunities of the Promised Land, but also an accurate memory of what Egypt was really like.

In addition, transition management often requires that the bridges connecting people to the past be burned. This is a ticklish business because it is important not to dishonor the past. To do so only makes those who once depended on it defensive. It is dangerous to try to make people recant what they once found meaningful, but to keep them from retreating, it may be necessary to break up groups that could serve as the rallying grounds for the adherents of the old order or terminate policies and procedures that keep the old ways alive.

One way to establish both a break and a continuity is to present the change as the natural outgrowth of some important part of the past. Roger Smith did that at General Motors when he initiated a sweeping program of changes in an organization that has been notoriously resistant to change: "I've heard people say, 'Oh, Mr. Sloan would be spinning in his grave if he knew what you were doing.' I say that's nuts. He'd be doing exactly what I'm doing. I really believe that."*

Sixth, creating new communication channels, and using them. Management needs to communicate constantly, saying things simply, and saying them over and over again. With confusion rampant, people have trouble understanding (sometimes even hearing) what they are being told. That difficulty is compounded when people who were supposed to pass on the information to those who report to them fail to do so. The neutral zone is full of such "failures," because information is worth a great deal in any organization where it is scarce. Hoarding information is one way of shoring up a position that is threatened by change. The supervisor doesn't tell his men about the deadline to apply for the new production team jobs; the middle manager doesn't tell her subordinates about the impending reorganization of their department; and the vice-president doesn't tell his unit managers about the delay in the merger. There are always specific reasons, but under the details they vary so little from organization to organization that one is forced to think that they are highly stylized excuses rather than explanations:

"I thought the staff already knew."

"There's no point in getting the employees upset until they have to know."

"The union will just get paranoid and claim we're out to get them again."

"I don't know why I forgot. I have so much on my mind these days . . ."

The results of blocked neutral-zone communications are also predictable: diminished trust, increased hostility, anxiety-producing rumors and a musical-chairs mentality in which the competition for a shrinking number of places escalates to the point where it becomes a full-time activity.

Seventh, protecting people in the neutral zone from further changes whenever possible. In a dynamic organizational environment, further changes are inevitable, of course, but some changes are optional and should be avoided. At a food-processing company where I helped to design an effective transition-management plan, a new company president took office in the midst of the transition between one technological system and another. When the work teams were still in limbo between the old technology and the new, he announced that the company would also convert to a new kind of packaging and a whole new way of preparing the food for packaging. The whole change effort was seriously jeopardized.

Eighth, monitoring the course of the changes carefully. In most organizations, one or more Transition Monitoring Teams have proved to be effective ways of ascertaining the state of the transition and keeping track of people and units, so that nobody falls through the cracks between what was and what will be. Such monitoring is seldom done adequately within the chain of command—even within the temporary authority structures of the Transition Management Group. Hierarchies are necessary to manage transition successfully, but they are not very good channels for disseminating information and are even worse at gathering it.

A far better group can be made up of people chosen from the various affected units and the different levels of the organization. This kind of a "diagonal slice" of the organization has saved a number of organizations I have worked with from serious problems. Transition Monitoring Teams are effective ways to learn about difficulties before they get large, to feed into the decision-making process suggestions from otherwise silent elements in the organization, and to act as an internal focus group within which to try out alternative plans or announcements. In a small organization, a single team may suffice; in a large one, they should be set up within each seriously affected unit.

Finally, educating people about this strange interim state called the neutral zone. Leaders must understand people's need for time to reorient themselves. Managers should understand why temporary structures and policies are necessary. Supervisors must understand what the neutral zone does to people, so that they do not simply apply more pressure when pressure no longer works. And the people themselves need to understand the neutral zone, so that they do not think that they have fallen afoul of a merely personal distress. Just because our culture lacks a clear conception of this dangerous but fertile gap, many people blame themselves or each other for the problems that occur there. In my Transition Management Seminars, I always find that even simply naming and describing the neutral zone elicits recognition and relief from participants.

What it takes to deal successfully with the anxieties and confusions that people feel in the neutral zone may seem a vicious circle;

to admit the anxiety and confusion is to blow the cover that their emotional security depends on. Worse yet, if no one else is talking, it can seem that no one else has these awful secrets. If no one else has such secrets, admitting them will only show that you don't belong in your position—that you are an impostor who has fooled people in the past but who is now unmasked. Talking about the feeling is a solution that looks worse than the problem.

But talk *is* the key to dealing with these anxieties, for once the self-doubts have surfaced in either individual or group discussion, they lose much of their power. People discover that they are not alone. They break out of what they have been experiencing as impossibly painful states of isolation and to find a companionship in the stormy waters of the neutral zone that they never experienced in the calm weather of "better times."

One of the things that an outsider can bring to an organization in the neutral zone is this perspective on the anxiety that many employees are sure to be feeling. (It is one thing to hear that your dismay is natural from an outsider who has no established stake in the present situation, and another to hear it from a superior who you know wants you to stay calm.) Something else that the outsider can bring is the status of being a safe listener. In most organizations where I work, I spend a good deal of time talking with people about what the neutral zone is doing to their sense of self-worth. Sometimes this is done individually, and sometimes it is done in groups. The group setting is more economical and also has the advantage of providing a place where people can give one another emotional support. But when individuals are highly placed or when the organizational culture penalizes self-disclosure too much, it can be more effective to work with people individually.

Not everyone can, or even should, let go of old defenses in the neutral zone. In some cases the anxiety is so great that in the end the individual's defenses against authentic self-awareness and self-disclosure are reinforced rather than relaxed. Such people pay a high cost for such "security." Often they begin to show signs of pathology, even though they formerly functioned adequately or even well. One cannot read the accounts of Nixon's last days in the White House without suspecting that this was happening in his case. One sees the same pattern in the fictional history of Captain

Queeg in *The Caine Mutiny* and in the real-life behaviors of thousands of departmental tyrants whose worlds begin to crumble when their external buttresses disappear during organizational change.

Such people would need more extensive and deeper-probing kinds of help than are likely to be available in an organizational setting, and they must usually be removed from their positions and responsibilities. Such help needs to be offered and delivered with great care, however, both for their sake and so that they do not become martyrs in the eyes of other sufferers. But when it is well handled, transfer or termination of such individuals leaves both them and the organization better off.

Few people require such treatment, however, for most of the time a chance to talk out the neutral-zone experience with a skilled outside listener or with a group of peers in a safe and controlled setting is enough to help a person get through the neutral zone's low-pressure area intact. Sometimes just knowing why one's old fears are coming back is enough, and so it definitely pays to educate people about what transition is and does.

As I said earlier, the breakdown of one's old reality in the neutral zone has a positive as well as a negative side. The same wilderness that frightened Moses's followers into idealizing the past and talking about returning to it was also the place where Jehovah appeared to Moses and gave him both a new vision of the future and a new set of cultural precepts to live by. On an individual level the same process of revelation happened to the young Sioux who was taken into the wilderness beyond his village where the guidance of parents and elders disappeared and an inner spirit guide took their place. That Native American wilderness experience was called by a name that captures the positive side of the neutral zone very well: the Vision Quest.

The Vision Quest aspect of the neutral zone has, itself, two different faces. On the one hand it represents a time-out, an experience of being away from the old system and the self that fitted in with it. In that time-out, the old reality can disintegrate and make way for the new. Life in that neutral-zone wilderness is a time of returning to basics, a time of cutting through all the apparent realities of the previous developmental phase, a time of returning to the bedrock of existence. The very emptiness that is the source of so much anxiety is also the precondition of the new vision.

On the other hand, the neutral-zone wilderness also provides an access to wisdom from those areas of consciousness that would be filtered out of awareness in the normal course of everyday life. In this time and place of insight and vision, all traditional societies developed rituals of passage to help people to become sensitized to the guidance that was available when everyday signals and situations disappeared. It is no wonder that the wilderness of the neutral zone has been regarded as a holy place by tribal cultures everywhere.

Arnold van Gennep was the first Western scholar to make sense out of passage rituals. In his book *Rites of Passage,* he demonstrated that traditional societies sent their members periodically into the wilderness, both to facilitate their passage from one state of being to another and to enable them to make contact with the kinds of inner guidance that were available there. As in the model of organizational transition being presented here, the ancient wisdom decreed that any profound change required the death of the identity that a person or group had had and the rebirth of another. The time in the neutral zone, on this model, was also a time of gestation before rebirth. As part of that gestation, the myths of the tribe's origins were recounted, and rituals that dramatized the creation of the world were enacted.*

Lest you worry that this is drifting away from the real world of the organization into the esoteric worlds of anthropology and mythology, reflect on how frequently and almost unconsciously people recall the acts of an organization's founders and early leaders whenever they are in the midst of transition. IBM draws on stories about Thomas Watson, Jr., Hewlett-Packard on stories about Bill Hewlett and Dave Packard, and generations of Americans have recalled the mythologized acts of George Washington whenever they stood at a difficult collective turning point.

The pattern that Van Gennep describes is validated in another way as well. Bowlby's studies of bereavement demonstrate that it is essential to go through an extended time of waiting before any real new beginning can be made.* An example: Warning against the temptation to have another child quickly to replace one that has died, Bowlby says that time is needed "to enable [the parents] to reorganize their image of the lost child and so retain it as a living memory distinct from any new child they may have." His words echo the folk wisdom that tells us that it is unwise to "marry on the rebound," for second unions made before one has had a chance to become emotionally free of the first have a high incidence of failure.

There are several different ways to look at this psychological need to return to nothingness before beginning anew. Bowlby emphasizes the way in which the nothingness extinguishes the old responses and expectations. Of the terrible emptiness that follows the more active stage of grieving, he writes:

> . . . such disorganization and the mood of depression that goes with it, though painful and perhaps bewildering, is none the less potentially adaptive. For until the patterns of behaviour that are organized for interactions that are no longer possible have been dismantled it is not possible for new patterns, organized for new interactions, to be built up . . . [But] because it is necessary to discard old patterns of thinking, feeling and acting before new ones can be fashioned, it is almost inevitable that a bereaved person should at times despair that anything can be salvaged and, as a result, fall into depression and apathy.

This is a memorable description and explanation of the neutral zone in its negative aspect. With the artist's instinct for the essential, Picasso said the same thing much more briefly: "Every act of creation is first of all an act of destruction."

Studies of creativity provide another way of looking at what is going on in the neutral zone. In several different ways, these studies tell the same story: Creative ideas, innovative designs, and new patterns of organization come from those areas of the inner world that are chaotic by ordinary standards. They come from those areas of the psyche that lie outside the familiar realms of thinking and feeling, areas that most of us experience with mild panic as confusing or even crazy. They come from areas that are largely closed off during the modes of functioning that we rely on when the organizational world is more or less stable.

What actually blocks most of us off from the creativity that we could exercise is our conceptual and perceptual rigidity. "Reality" is defined by how we have seen and understood things in the past, and it is those old perceptions and conclusions that stand in the way of seeing them differently in the future. It is only when we can let go of those ways of seeing and understanding and live without such baggage for a while that we are likely to come up with any solution or outlook that deserves the term "creative."

The creative person is not so much one with great talent as it is one who can endure the confusions and anxieties of the neutral zone long enough for a fundamental reorganization of his or her experience to take place. In many organizations, deep and lasting change is aborted simply because the people involved could not bear the chaos and uncertainty about what was emerging long enough to let it take shape. We must, therefore, add a tenth key to neutral-zone management to the nine given earlier: Be patient. All the supports and clarifications recommended earlier are in a sense simply the framework to contain the creative chaos and to make patience possible.

In my Transition Management Seminars, a question always arises at this point: Granted that we must be patient . . . isn't there *something* we can do to encourage the creative reshaping of structure and strategy in the neutral zone? There are at least three things that can be done:

You can provide opportunities for the organizational leadership and affected employees to step back and take stock of where things really stand, collectively and personally, and what they want to do about that. The old tribal societies were right in their belief that neutral zone is the place where one may be granted a compelling new vision for the future.

You can also resist the temptation to silence dissident voices and seek unanimity. This can be hard to do, because when things are clearly coming apart, it sounds logical and is certainly natural to use any common ground that can be discovered to rebuild the lost cohesion. But it is important, nonetheless, to encourage constantly —and especially during the stock-taking recommended above—divergent thinking, to encourage the tendency of people to march to their own drummers. It is true enough that the group needs to preserve itself, but innovativeness and creativity begin in the minds of individuals who are seeing through their own eyes and thinking for themselves.

Finally, you can help people identify and understand fully the unmet needs that may be inherent in the problematical situation that brought the old reality to an end. You can help them to see how these unanswered and seemingly unanswerable questions represent opportunities that are created by change. For change always creates new opportunity, and in the neutral zone it becomes visible. It is in these strange gaps between past and future that organizational innovation is likeliest to take place. In *The Change Masters,* Rosabeth Moss Kanter remarks how often structural and technical innovations take place during reorganizations or changes in leadership.* These in-between times are cracks in the organizational reality in which new life can take root.

As the British historian Arnold J. Toynbee pointed out fifty years ago, the process of social renewal has always been associated with journeys into boundary states.* In his *A Study of History,* Toynbee surveyed the histories of twenty-six great civilizations and concluded that their times of renewal and growth coincided with two factors. First, they all came to a point of crisis in which some external change or internal development challenged the old order to the point where it broke down—in our terms, they came to an ending. Second, individuals or groups from the society which had been challenged by change disengaged themselves at that point from the world of action and withdrew into the wilderness or some other form of solitude which embodied the psychological no-man's-land of the neutral zone.

Everything that Toynbee says about societies applies to organizations as well. Organizational "withdrawals and returns" exist already in embryonic form in the common practice of taking top management on a retreat (sometimes even a retreat in a wilderness setting) during times of challenging change. These retreats are an opportunity for the collective stock-taking that was recommended above. At such retreats, brainstorming, metaphorical problem-solving techniques, lateral thinking, and other tactics are often used to encourage the kind of divergent and creative thought that is appropriate to the neutral zone. These retreats are modern organizational equivalents of the quest for a vision that took a Sioux boy or girl out into the emptiness of the high plains, and by being more consciously designed as Vision Quests, such retreats can be an even more useful than they usually are.

Because they are so useful to an organization in transition, I want to describe these retreats in a little more detail. They begin with some kind of public recognition—verbal or even ceremonial—of both the external, collective endings that have taken place and the internal, personal ones that the external ones have caused. Since people may be denying the impact of these endings, it may take some time for them to recognize and acknowledge how significant they are. Participants are encouraged to recall and retell stories that catch the flavor of the positive things that they and others have lost, as well as to think of stories that illustrate those elements of the vanishing situation that they are glad to let go of. Such a story-telling session turns easily into something like a wake for the organization's past, and it has the same goal of focusing feeling so that it can be then set aside. As with a wake, food and drink help the recollection and recounting along. Typically this phase ends in the evening, and after it everyone goes off to sleep.

The next day of the neutral-zone retreat is spent exploring the experience of being in between realities. The celebratory meal and the rich talk of the night before give way to a more spartan fare (or even fasting) and to periods of quiet, as the participants feel what it is to live with the emptiness of a time without tight schedules and definitive events. Experiences are planned that give participants new views of their familiar organizational reality. The goal is to encourage what Edward de Bono calls "lateral thinking," the creative exploration of situations that discovers new possibilities—collective and individual—in circumstances where people have limited themselves by being unable to see things in any but one dead-end way.*

Such a retreat should have an off-site setting and an informal atmosphere that encourages people to let go of habitual behavior and conventional (de Bono would call it) "vertical" thinking. The schedule should include periods of unstructured time in which people are encouraged to be alone with their thoughts—thoughts that they are encouraged to record in some way for future use. The activities of the neutral-zone segment of the retreat should include exercises that assist people in using their minds in ways that may be unfamiliar to them: drawing, metaphorical thinking, and visualizing.

Getting fresh perspective on the present can also be encouraged by activities that put participants into unfamiliar roles and situations. One of the most effective retreats of this sort that I ever attended required a group of senior corporate officers to cook a complete meal from a Julia Child cookbook. I'll never forget finding one executive alone in the kitchen with an egg in his hand and the beginnings of a chocolate cake in a bowl in front of him. "It says 'Separate the egg,' Bill," the man said with a note of panic in his voice. "What the hell *from?*"

The experience of being completely confused and inept is one that most executives go to great lengths to avoid, and in so doing they often fail to explore the very areas where new ideas and alternative lines of action might be discoverable. The person who cannot cross the boundaries of familiarity and self-control is doomed to follow the same worn paths over and over again to the same unfortunate destinations.

Because it represents a break from the organization's ordinary reality, the organizational "withdrawal and return" experience is usually best planned and led by an outsider. But it will not accomplish its goal without the blessings and participation of the organization's leaders on an equal footing with everyone else. Toward the end of the retreat, the external facilitator should help the participants plan the best way to bring back to the everyday organizational world some of their discoveries and commitments to action.

The neutral zone is a time when the formalities of a stable hierarchy feel burdensome and actually hinder the necessary business of gestating new patterns of thought and behavior. One of the functions of the withdrawal-and-return experience to create a sense of being in the same boat that is almost impossible to create at any other time. In *The Ritual Process,* Victor Turner shows that what he calls the "liminal" phase of the passage ritual (which we are calling the "neutral zone") is characterized by a denial or even a reversal of the hierarchies that are normally held to be important.* Contrasting a liminal situation with the more stable states that come before and after it, he says that a number of differences are typical:

STABLE STATE	LIMINAL STATE
Inequality	Equality
Status	Absence of status
Systems of nomenclature	Anonymity
Distinctions of clothing	Uniform clothing
Care for personal appearance	Disregard for personal appearance

The neutral zone is a time when, as the more superficial and external signs of social roles disappear, people begin to question who they really are and where they are going. It is a natural time of realignment, and for it to succeed, people need to be encouraged to take stock of things professionally and personally as well as organizationally. It is important, at such a time, to help self-discovery along so that people don't get too bewildered. There are a number of life-planning exercises that can help people in transition to understand themselves better and to study their options, and to realize that opportunities still exist. (See chapter 9, "Making Change Work for You" for a way to explore such opportunities.)

This kind of life and career replanning should not be limited to top management; it is a good thing to offer it in seminar form to a broad range of the people affected by a significant organizational change. Such a seminar should not focus on job-hunting skills or promotion opportunities within the organization. They should be built around two skill-building activities: strategies to understand oneself better and to set one's priorities more clearly, and strategies for identifying unmet needs within the organization and creating new ways to meet them.

People sometimes discover that change provides a good time to leave the organization. But it is more common for people to discover, through this kind of a seminar, that change provides a good chance to make a transition within the organization—to let go of an outlived plan and take on more appropriate challenges. In fact, it is when people feel disoriented and trapped by change, not when they can see previously unperceived opportunities, that they are likely to walk out of a job and a career.

The neutral zone makes heavy demands upon a leader, for it is a time for highly visible, supportive leadership that communicates a sense of evolving purpose. The leader who is just as confused as everyone else is no help, but neither is the leader who has all the answers and is only waiting for others to recognize that fact. As with many neutral zone issues, Moses provides a good model: climbing the mountain to get the vision and coming back down and sharing it; walking around and talking to the people in front of their tents; reminding them why they are out there in the desert and why the strange but attractive "gods" of the quick fix won't work. Neutral-zone leadership alternately pushes and draws people along the wilderness path toward the new beginning. It is the original Management by Walking Around.

If all of this sounds a little strange and unbusinesslike, that may simply show why so few businesses manage transition successfully. The neutral zone is such an unfamiliar and frightening place to most organizational leaders, that they rush their people through it as quickly as possible or retreat from it into a past that can only be kept alive by heroic measures. Or else the leaders themselves get lost in the wilderness and are deserted by their followers. In all those cases, the organization fails to make the real transition which the change set into motion.

On both the individual and the collective level, the neutral zone provides a chance to make deep changes that go far beyond the reestablishment of a functioning system. It is tempting to settle for the latter, but if that is done a precious opportunity has been lost. The neutral zone chaos after a significant ending is like the scene after a natural disaster; things have come apart, and they can either be patched back together again or rebuilt from the ground up. Many cities owe their present beauty to such major rebuilding efforts after disaster.

An internationally known expert on disaster relief, Frederick Cuny, has made a career out of helping cities, provinces, and whole countries orchestrate the difficult task of total reconstruction. Rather than focusing relief efforts on temporary and superficial assistance, Cuny has developed ways of working with local groups to transform the damaged and destroyed neighborhoods into something far better than it was before. "If you give [disaster victims] a tent, they ask for other goodies," he says bluntly. "If you give them hammer and nails, they build something."*

Properly managed, the neutral zone is where the real gift of transition will be received. As Henry David Thoreau said, "Corn grows in the night." The real transformation from something outmoded to something adequate for the future takes place below the surface at times when the casual observer might think that little was happening. The neutral zone is where the old behaviors and attitudes are laid to rest and where the new behaviors and attitudes begin to take shape. So leading people through the neutral zone successfully is the key to the larger task of bringing an organization through a period of change with new vigor and a new sense of purpose.

5: Making the New Beginning

He has half the deed done, who has made a new beginning.

Horace, *Epistles*

Pacific Mutual Life Insurance Company is the West's oldest mutual insurance company and the twenty-eighth largest of the nation's 2,100 life insurance companies. Founded in 1868 by pioneering industrialists Charles Crocker and Leland Stanford, it followed traditional paths until it ran into trouble during the recession of 1982. What had always worked well was not working anymore, and it was clearly time to let go of the old way of doing things. The company had come to an ending.*

Pacific Mutual cut its work force by a third and undertook the kind of deep self-study that an organizational neutral zone makes possible. Chairman Walter Gerken and President Harry Bubb began holding meetings with groups of employees; they also held a three-day retreat for the thirty-two top executives in the company. As a result of the discussions, a new organizational identity began to emerge: a multifaceted financial services company, rather than an insurance company as such. As this new identity became better defined, a new organizational design took shape: a cluster of six strategic business units, each focused on a particular type of financial service for a particular market. To make clear the implications of these far-reaching organizational changes "Life Insurance Company" was dropped from the corporate name, and Pacific Mutual was poised to make a fresh start.

Where Pacific Mutual differed from many organizations that were facing comparable challenges in the early eighties was in its recognition of the importance of managing transition as well as change and its recognition that a new start must be converted into a real *beginning* if it is to breathe new life into an organization. The leadership at Pacific Mutual recognized, that is, that new structural designs and new company names are simply empty shells, unless they are filled with human effort and intention. So they set about the task of helping their people to come out of the confusion of the neutral zone with new attitudes, a new sense of purpose, and a new repertoire of behavior. Their tactics provide a useful model of managing a new beginning.

Early in 1984 the twelve-person Management Committee redefined Pacific Mutual's mission in the light of the new challenges and opportunities of the marketplace so that everyone could understand the company's new purpose, and so that the company's top managers were deeply committed to the mission. Next a booklet was produced that spelled out the structure, the general policies, and the cultural values that would be required in the restructured company. (Interestingly, one of the five core values was *change.* "Change is the vehicle that brings us to the future," the booklet said. "And like the future, which must be invited and shaped, change must be harnessed and utilized." Much of the effectiveness of the new organization has been based on its acceptance of the reality of continual change and its development of ways to deal constructively with it.)

Then dozens of two-hour "Culture, Vision, Values" meetings were set up with groups of twenty to forty, so that every employee at the company headquarters had the chance to talk about the new beginning with the company's leaders and to see them modeling the new core values of Openness, Risk Taking, Accountability, Goal Orientation—and Change. The same "Culture, Vision, Values" framework became the basis for a thirty-minute video that was distributed to the company's seventy field offices and was used by company recruiters to help them attract new employees who shared the organization's values. Like the meetings, the video spread the message that the new values were not just the preferred operating style of the company leadership, but were the qualities that would be necessary to meet the challenges of the changes that the company was facing.

After that, the Training and Development Department presented a number of two-and-a-half-day seminars on the Process of Change in which employees whose situations were being particularly disrupted were educated about the three phases of transition. These seminars were more than didactic exercises, for they recapitulated the three stages of transition experientially in such a way that the participants could recognize what it was time to let go of individually and collectively, how they were being affected by the chaos of the neutral zone, and what a new beginning might mean for them personally.

At the same time, company publications began to spotlight the efforts of people whose departments were most successful in the transition-management process: "Find out what San Diego Group Benefits manager did to motivate her office staff to win the Model Office Award," suggested a front page editorial in the company newsletter. Such publicity provided people with models to imitate, as well as providing public recognition for the efforts of those who led the way in putting the new values into practice.

When all this had been done, a new motto was announced: GOWI . . . "Get On With It." A week for two in Hawaii was offered as a prize to the employee who could come up with the best symbol for that new action-oriented attitude. This campaign was felt by some employees to be a little corny, but it succeeded in drawing many previously uninvolved people into the transition management effort, and it effectively signaled that the time had come to stop talking and start acting in the new ways.

Finally, when the new company structure was in place and functioning, Pacific Mutual rented the ballroom of a large new hotel, and threw an enormous party for everyone in the company. There were reminiscences about the past and predictions about the future. There was a fine dinner and there was dancing. And at a cost of several million dollars, everyone in the whole company got a two-hundred-dollar bonus on the spot! (The original dream, which had been to bring a cash-filled armored car to the party and pass out hundred dollar bills, had to be abandoned for security reasons—though everyone agreed that would have been a nice touch.)

Pacific Mutual's way of managing a beginning would not fit every organization—and it was not without its own internal critics. But by the end of 1985, the company had reversed its decline, was thriving in its new organizational form, had grown to be the tenth-largest company in California (as measured in annual revenue), had launched still another strategic business unit, and had (not coincidentally) been named Company of the Year by the Orange County chapter of the American Society for Training and Development. More important, a work force that had been disoriented and demoralized had come out of a critically important transition with new commitment to new goals and a new style of working together. Pacific Mutual had managed to make a very good new beginning.

Any new organizational form, whether it is a manufacturing system or a product or a business strategy, is based on some seminal idea which is, in Charles Lofy's words, "the organizing principle for constellating the new energy that has been released by giving up the old form."* But just getting the idea and proclaiming it is not enough, although that is often what leaders think that they are supposed to do. The new idea will only work if it is presented when the people who must make the new beginning have been in the neutral zone long enough to be (as Robert Frost once said) "lost enough to find themselves."

It is the gift of the wise leader to be able to intuit when people are in that state of readiness. There is, unfortunately, no way to test that readiness objectively, but certain indications are worth looking for. The first one is evidence that people really have given up on the past. They stop bargaining and chasing after simple solutions, and develop a somber realism about the insufficiency of the old answers. The second indication is an upturn in the mood from one of grieving over what has been lost to one of interest in alternatives. This is not the anxious search for answers that may have been going on for a long time. It is something quieter and solider than that—a readiness to consider something really new and different.

An untimely attempt to launch a beginning can be worse than merely ineffective, since it can abort the transition itself. Timing explains the importance of something that good managers do instinctively: They withold their own new idea until their people are convinced that the old ideas are no longer working. They "sell the problem" before they try to "sell the solution." In fact, wise managers find that if they put adequate energy into selling the problem, the solution needs relatively little selling.

Many image-conscious, positive-thinking managers and leaders, however, hate to acknowledge that there are any problems. Negative evaluation of how things are going is relegated to the back rooms and the car pools. More openly expressed, it is taken to be a sign of a lack of confidence or negative thinking. Such managers fear that if a problem is acknowledged, it will reflect badly on them. After all, the American success story promises that in a well-run organization, things just keep getting better and better—that the old becomes new without any break or relinquishment.

Such thinking is not only unrealistic. It also blinds the organization's management to the fact that the kinds of ideas that are necessary to create a new beginning do not *solve* the problems of the present. Rather they *redefine* the present's problems. Nowhere is this truer than in regard to the new ideas that lie behind the redefinition of an organization's mission.

An example: Oshkosh, Inc., the maker of old-time work clothes, found its growth blocked by a shrinking market. Blue-collar jobs were disappearing slowly, and fashion no longer encouraged a back-to-the-earth look. As long as Oshkosh saw itself as the maker of tough work clothes, that identity tied it to a very uncertain future and a widespread feeling of being victimized by change. But if Oshkosh could re-identify itself as the maker of a particular clothing form (overalls), it was free to play with other ways that that product might look and other markets that might be served. If you have seen children's tiny, flowered "designer overalls," you know the result. The company can no longer keep up with orders and has had to subcontract some of its orders out to other suppliers.

This redefinition of one's main business is far easier to do in a small organization that is focused on relatively few products or services. USX (né U.S. Steel) and General Motors are naturally having a far harder time of it, although the difference is not one of kind but of complexity. Because the example of a small organization makes the function of the germinal idea clearer than does a big organization, let me offer another, this time from the field of education.

Oregon's Marylhurst College was one of the country's many small women's liberal arts colleges that was on the verge of going out of business in the early seventies. Most students wanted to go to coeducational colleges, and fewer and fewer of them wanted to go to little religious institutions staffed by aging nuns. Yet there was an increase in one type of student: the adult woman, often middle-aged, with rich life experience but without recent academic experience. After shrinking enrollments had brought it to the edge of bankruptcy, Marylhurst redefined itself as a college for such women (and later their male counterparts) and transformed its curriculum, its schedules, and its policies to fit its new purpose. Career and life planning became a basic element in the course of study, rather than something one did privately after graduation, when one couldn't find a job. Issues of meaning and value, classic midlife questions, animated every course, from music to biology to economics. The basic teaching style changed, for teacher and student no longer differed very much in life-experience. The result: A dying institution was reborn and today thrives, in an environment that has destroyed many of its former counterparts and competitors.

"In the Beginning is the Idea." That is a fair enough statement of what Oshkosh and Marylhurst did, and it fits the experience of the "conceptual" people who usually think up such ideas. But within any organization there are many valuable people who do not instinctively respond to ideas. They find ideas too hypothetical until they have been fleshed out into full-scale "visions" of the organizational future—word pictures of how things will work and feel, of what kind of an organization it will be and how it differs from others like it. The envisioners are critical to a new beginning, because they take a germinal idea and can expand it into an emotionally engaging picture of the organization's future that will capture people's imaginations.

There are still others within the organization who find visions too imaginary. They are dreams, pie in the sky, make-believe. If there are going to be changes, these people want a step-by-step plan to show how a vision is going to be realized. They complain that the big picture looks terrific, but that the details and the structure are what make you or break you. These detail-minded people are critical to a new beginning, for without them the artist's rendering will not become the kind of working drawing of the structure that builders need.

And there is a fourth type of person who agrees that the plan is more important than the vision, but who finds the logical steps too impersonal. Such employees want to know who's going to do what and what their relation to others will be in the finished design. They want to know who's going to be in charge and what the expectations are going to be and how disagreements are going to be handled. This fourth type is concerned with how the people are going to relate to one another, and their concern is essential in planning a new beginning because without it the finished product can be unworkable.

We will return to these four basic temperaments or personality styles in chapter 7 and will see there that they are not simply theoretical constructs but are well-tested and useful ways to categorize how people perceive the world around them and turn those perceptions into action. I mention the four temperaments here to suggest why there is no one single key to managing a new beginning. What is critical to bringing one person out of the neutral zone is not nearly so effective with the person's office mate.

When you come to the new beginning, it is absolutely necessary to have a multidimensional plan that involves communication, leadership, training, incentives, and ritual. Successful beginnings depend on effective communication, just as successful endings and neutral zones do. But the communication is somewhat different in this third phase of transition from what it was in the first two. The ending required information-based communication that told what was going to happen, when it was going to happen, and why it was going to happen. The neutral zone required communication that provided people with a sense that someone was looking out for them during a very difficult time and that a process of clarification was going on that would in time provide the organization with a new direction. The communications required by a new beginning are less informational or supportive than evocative. Such communications depict the new organizational world that is going to come out of the transition. They do so with different emphases, in different people's words, using different media, in general and in particular—and again and again, for this communication is seeking to convey a whole new picture of things, and it is extremely difficult for the audience to see such a new pattern clearly.

The seed idea of the new organization needs to be explained, because some people respond most readily to ideas. They will go to work developing its implications in specific situations, sometimes in areas too small and specific to be covered by any plan. The idea of first-rate fast service is at the heart of everything that makes McDonald's such a successful enterprise. The idea of inexpensive, well-designed, and reliable transportation shaped the old VW Beetle and the company that rose out of war's rubble to build it. A similar idea, applied this time to computing, led to the Apple II series of computers and to the personal computer industry in general. So, the question is: *What is the new* idea *that lies at the heart of the new beginning?*

And next, what is the new organization that is going to put this idea into practice? What is your picture of how products or services are going to be created and delivered, how the producers and the customers are going to be treated, who is going to make the decisions? What is your vision of the new organization?

Then, how is that vision going to be realized? What is going to happen? When? In what order? How are present activities going to be coordinated with new activities? What training will be needed to staff the new roles, and how is that going to be provided?

Finally, where is everyone going to fit? What are the new roles going to look like? Where will I fit, and where will you fit? Who is my boss going to be, and what will his or her expectations be? How are you going to find the right place for each person and insure that everyone has a sense of "belonging" in the new organization?

These different questions lend themselves naturally to different communication strategies. Memos and bulletin-board notices are good ways to announce the details of a plan, but they cannot convey the vision of the new organization nor reassure people that their interests are being taken seriously. A videotaped statement by the CEO can reassure people or describe the idea from which the new beginning sprang, but it is a poor way to explain the details of a plan.

Remember too that communication is complete only when the originator of the message gets it back again as it has been understood by the receiver. There has been no communication if what is heard differs from what was said. In a manufacturing plant where I set up a transition management plan, the communications (which had been all written before I began) had to be translated into Spanish for the largely Latino work force. There were serious misunderstandings that hampered plans for the new beginning, however, and it was not until well after the fact that the Anglo managers discovered that their translator had twisted things around considerably in rendering them into another language. "Labor intensive jobs" had become "much work that is very hard," and "more rewarding jobs" had become "jobs that pay more." But it does not take a literal language gap to create misunderstandings. Any differences between the worlds of the speaker and the listener can do that, so wise managers constantly check how accurately they have been heard.

Since they themselves are quite capable of misunderstanding, managers need to examine their own impressions too. I recall the merger of two small technology companies in which the new management went to great lengths to prepare answers to all the questions that they expected employees to have. In preparation for an all-hands question and answer session, the president of the new company boned up on the new retirement policies, projected employment levels, plans for restructuring and for the integration of two product lines. It turned out that the two issues that most concerned the employees were whether everyone would get the same color ID badge (one company had white badges, and the other used gold for the managers and blue for the hourlies), and when employees from the smaller company could start using the larger company's picnic ground. Before you begin to talk, find out what the listeners want to learn.

One of the first things that a manager will hear from people who are launching a new beginning is that the old pattern of responsibilities doesn't fit anymore. Some people have very little to do in the new situation, while other people have picked up so many new responsibilities that they are completely overwhelmed. This problem is even more severe if the organization has lost employees in the course of its transition or if the same group of people is trying to keep an existing operation going at the same time it is launching a new operation.

Some managers take on this task of reallocating responsibilities as though it were a solo act, but that is usually a mistake for at least three reasons. First, the people are likely to be feeling the need of some way to regain control over their work lives, and the manager who redefines everyone's responsibilities misses an opportunity to give the people back such control. Second, people have trouble settling into new roles until they have adjusted them for personal fit. One person thrives on shared responsibilities and another can't stand them. To the extent that it is possible, such preferences should be respected; no matter how hard a manager tries to do that, he or she simply cannot make responsibilities fit as completely as people themselves can. And finally, the people themselves probably know more about what has to be done and who's best at each aspect of the common task than the manager does.

The manager's situation is like that of a landscape architect who was asked by a university to design a way to keep the students on the paved paths that crisscrossed the campus.* The university had already made oral and written announcements of the Keep Off the Grass policy. They had followed the announcements with signs on the lawns themselves and had instituted punishments against those who continued to walk on the grass. When that had failed, the universities security officers began issuing citations to students who were caught crossing the lawns.

Like many managers, the architect found himself in a situation where all the effort was being spent on gaining compliance with a preestablished plan. The architect did not accept the idea that his job was to keep the students on the paths or to determine logically a better pattern of paths. Instead, he requested that the grounds crew not clear the snow from the campus one winter. Within a few weeks, a perfectly functional network of footpaths appeared in the snow. In places they followed the old paved routes, but elsewhere they cut across what had been open lawn. When the people themselves had produced a clear and workable pattern, he staked out their routes and when the snow melted in the spring had them paved. Harnessing the natural forces within the situation itself and interfering only to insure that those forces could leave a clear and reliable pattern to be followed in the future, the architect was a model manager of new beginnings.

Beginnings call for a clarification of responsibilities in other areas besides those of ongoing operations: for example, in task forces that are trying to set up a new unit or launch a new undertaking. The official positions occupied by such people seldom define adequately who should do what in an *ad hoc* grouping, so the task force itself needs to be very explicit in assigning responsibilities. In so doing, they should remember that there are different degrees of responsibility. Some "responsibility" is that of actually deciding what is to be done; some is that of approving whatever is going to be done; some is that of carrying out the plans; and some is simply that of staying informed and passing that information on to others. If these different aspects of responsibility are not kept separate, too many people will be doing some things, no one will be doing others, and people who need to know what is going on will be afraid to ask for fear of being told to roll up their sleeves and get to work.

As responsibilities are redefined in the light of the needs of the new situation, training begins to be needed—though a more accurate way of putting it would be to say that training begins to be requested or resisted, offered or refused. Organizations beginning anew have few resources that are more important, yet more often misused, than training. Anyone concerned with a new beginning needs to consider these issues.

First the planners and managers of organizational change need to be reminded that new skills and knowledge are required by any new role or new responsibilities. It is surprising how often organizations pay a great deal of money for new equipment and refuse to pay a little money to train people to use it properly. Similarly, people are promoted from sales or the shop floor into a management role, with a great deal riding on their success, and are given no training whatsoever in management skills. Organizations also frequently shift people from R & D to manufacturing or from manufacturing to sales as part of a reorganization that is meant to improve effectiveness, and then offer them no training in the basic knowledge required to be competent in their new field. (It is, of course, equally common for organizations to assign the responsibility for managing critical organizational transitions to individuals who have no understanding of what transition is or how to manage it.) In each of these cases, there are training programs that could save the organization time, money, and stress. So the first question that anyone who is responsible for the success of a new beginning needs to ask is: What new skills or new knowledge will be required of employees to make the new beginning work—and what kind of training would supply what is needed?

The second kind of training that most new beginnings requires is training in seeing and understanding things in new contexts.* Take as an example the case of a computer company with a marketing problem. The company has an excellent line of basic computers, and it provides a wide range of services and secondary products to enhance those computers. But its culture has always emphasized innovative design and fine technical service rather than sales and marketing. As a result, it has a wonderful group of service technicians, but its sales force is weak. In the past, the products and service were well enough known by longtime users to sell themselves, but in today's marketplace competitors have overtaken the company with big promotional campaigns and aggressive sales staffs.

Skill-based training might begin by identifying the skills and strategies that effective salespeople use and then teach them to the second-rate sales force. But context-based training might well take a different tack, by bypassing the question of specific skills and instead reeducating the technicians about their new function as "technical consultants" within the company. They are taught to think of their job as that of helping clients be more successful by providing them with more effective computer assistance, rather than as that of being repair technicians. That more effective assistance from the computer may involve an upgrade to a new model or some peripheral equipment to do new tasks; it may involve a whole network of computers, or a hook-in to the company phone system. More effective assistance will result in sales, but sales will be a by-product of a new way of serving the customer. Of course, more effective assistance with using the computer will also continue to include fixing it when it breaks. But "fixing" is now only part of a larger purpose. And that larger purpose redefines a problem in such a way that it becomes an opportunity.

Context-based training has many advantages. It does not try to spell out in advance just what actions will be necessary to reach the goal. Such prescribed procedures seldom work as well in the customer's office as they do in the training seminar. What is needed instead is a clear sense of one's new goal and a sensitivity to the client's need. Former technicians who have been taught sales techniques spend too much of their time trying to remember them and deciding which ones to use in each situation. A procedure that is learned detail by detail is only as strong as its weakest step, and it has to be reinforced by rote practice and brush-up courses.

But recontextualizing programs do not depend on retained information, and they are naturally reinforced by the results each time that they succeed. Technicians who have learned to see their activities in the new consultative context simply think "How can I help this person?" They use their imagination rather than their memory, and they build a new self-image on the basis of the results they achieve rather than the competence they demonstrate in class.

For all their advantages, context-based programs work best when they are supplemented by training in skills and strategies. When you ask the question that you were taught to ask in the sales seminar, it may be a mechanical act, but if it is combined with context-based training it will initiate a dialogue which will teach you things about the client and about yourself. Skill- and strategy-based training also reinforces context-based training if you are one of those planners who isn't really comfortable unless he knows what he's supposed to do next. Even if you are not such a person you can benefit from studying your desired role behaviorally, for the weakness of your naturally more intuitive temperament is always going to be that you think impressionistically and therefore may have trouble identifying the particular parts of what you do that need to be improved.

The second question about training that anyone responsible for a new beginning needs to ask, therefore, is: How could this new beginning be strengthened if some of the people involved could see or understand their function differently—and what kind of training could I provide to help them do that?

Training people to do things a new way will count for little if their reward system makes it more advantageous for them to keep behaving in the old way. The current jargon for this is "incentivizing" the change—which is a term only a little less awful than its opposite, which you must avoid: "disincentivizing" it. Unless someone changes them, both the formal reward system (promotions and income) and the subtler pattern of informal incentives (praise, interesting temporary assignments, training opportunities) are going to promote the behavior and attitudes that were necessary to yesterday's circumstances. This natural brake on transition may well go unnoticed, however, for it is so deeply embedded in people's habits and expectations that it may not be very visible. But it is common for an organization to announce new policies and new procedures and then undermine them by literally and figuratively making it pay to do things the old way.

This often happens when an organization moves into a new field where different qualities and behaviors need to be rewarded. When Fairchild moved into microelectronics, for example, it failed to adjust its compensation system and denied stock options to the engineers in its semiconductor division in California's Silicon Valley, where such incentives were commonplace. The result was a loss of the very talent that had made Fairchild an early leader in this field, a loss that culminated when Dr. Robert Noyce left to launch a little firm named Intel.

Although it may well be necessary ultimately to revamp the compensation and benefits system totally to reinforce the new beginning, there are many smaller moves that can pay off handsomely:

• one-time bonuses for the early exemplars of the new skills and the new style required by the transition

• special rewards for people who create effective ways of removing roadblocks to change

• public recognition of people who are willing to let go of old perks and benefits, when those stand in the way of a new beginning

Some organizations develop formal awards to recognize people who model their new values especially well. Versatec, Inc., gives "You Want It When?" awards to employees whose efforts are especially noteworthy, and at Vector Corporation they use "Attaboy" awards in a similar way.*

Ritual and other symbolic expressions are important ways to focus attention on the pattern beneath the surface details at any stage of transition. In the first phase of transition, ritual and symbolism can give substance to the otherwise amorphous sense of loss; in the second phase of transition they give people a way to grasp and find meaning in the confusing "wilderness" of the neutral zone. During a beginning, which is transition's final phase, ritual and symbolism are effective when they are used in a much more narrowly focused way to dramatize the new expectations and the values that underlie them.

General Bill Creech used symbolism effectively in his six-year revitalization effort when he was the commander of the Air Force's Tactical Air Command. Faced with shockingly high rates of mechanical failures, substandard levels of flying time, and an increasing number of crashes, Creech decided to focus on one main functional issue and one main organizational issue: maintenance and centralization. The story is a complex one that deserves to be better known, but in essence he reversed twenty years of centralizing efforts by pushing the authority and responsibility for decisions and results to the lowest possible level of his organization and then built self-contained teams to carry out the efforts at that level.

At every turn, this effort was ritualized and symbolized. Technicians who had always before been assigned to impersonal labor pools at big air bases were reassigned to flight squadrons with names like the Buccaneers or the Black Falcons. They topped off their mechanics' outfits with squadron baseball caps and were assigned to specific aircraft for which they were personally responsible and on which they were encouraged to do what had previously been forbidden—to paint their names, just as pilots did. (Creech also used incentives, for he ruled that any squadron that met its performance goals ahead of schedule could have an extra three-day weekend.)

Many beginnings are so large and far-reaching that it might seem as though one could not begin until everyone is fully committed to the goal and agreed on the steps. A great deal of what is currently being written about organizational change talks about "aligning" everyone, and uses arrows pointing in the same direction to illustrate this idea.

Yet such unanimity, like the perfect vacuum, does not exist in the real world. Commitment to something new is always incomplete and provisional, and groups within the organization may continue to oppose a new beginning until it is well established. The very image of "alignment" is somewhat misleading, since people aren't iron filings in a magnetic field but members of groups with interests that may be undermined by even the most important and best-managed change. A better image is one in which there are two or more different patterns of alignment that are polarized within an organization. Destroying the polarity is a less workable approach than redefining the situation in a way that shifts lines along which the situation is polarized.

This is what happens in electoral politics all the time. A losing coalition does not suddenly convert its opponents. Rather it redefines the situation in ways that serve both its values and the concerns of some other important parts of the electorate. Party A, which has won the support of only 40 percent of the voters by its ideology may capture 60 percent of them by showing that the opposition is dishonest. A company that is losing a price war with its competition may begin to win back customers if it redefines the issue by arguing successfully that "real value" depends on quality rather than price. Management and labor, opponents within many organizations, may become collaborators against an overseas opponent when the arena is redefined as the international marketplace. Yet even when these reorientations of conflict are very successful, they are not total. And anyone who waits for total alignment or neglects other important strategies in hopes of achieving it is making a serious mistake.

To push for complete commitment to a total change is self-defeating for another reason as well. Many new beginnings are overwhelmingly large and take discouragingly long to implement. Whether it is little St. Cabrini's hospital in Seattle trying to launch a new program for the treatment of eating disorders or gigantic AT&T trying to get itself out of the wilderness and make a new beginning, the prospect of something large and new makes most people feel increasingly intimidated as they learn more of what it will involve. Challenges activate people only up to a point; beyond that point (in psychologist Karl Weick's words) "people find it difficult to learn a novel response, to brainstorm, to concentrate, to resist old categories, to perform complex responses, to delegate, and to resist information that supports positions they have taken."

Since those behaviors are the very ones essential to making a successful new beginning, it is very important to overcome the numbing effects of an overwhelming task. The main strategy for doing this is to break down the overall objective into smaller and more easily achievable steps. Such steps activate rather than inhibit effort, and their achievement reinforces that effort and makes further steps easier. Such achievements also encourage support and discourage opposition from outside. Intentionally planned, they represent what Weick has called the "Small Wins Strategy."*

The Environmental Protection Agency's early days provide an instructive example of the Small Wins Strategy. Whereas many agencies of the late sixties and early seventies set about changing the world in one stroke, William Ruckelshaus, the first EPA administrator, played down his directive to clean up the whole environment and set instead more modest goals. As Tom Peters tells it,

> He discovered some obscure 80-year-old legislation that permitted him to go after some cities on water pollution. He took advantage of the legislation, effectively narrowing his practical agenda for the first year or two to "getting started on water pollution." On day one of the agency's formal existence, Ruckelshaus announced five major lawsuits against major American cities. The impact was electrifying. The homework had been meticulously done. Noticeable progress was made quickly. It formed the beachhead for a long series of successes and distinguished EPA from most of its sister agencies.

Does this mean that big, formal plans should be abandoned in favor of these pragmatic moves? Not at all. But it does mean that the implementation plan for any significant new beginning needs to be an interweaving of two themes rather than one. The first theme is the whole vision and the path toward its realization, as they are conceived logically and imaginatively. The second theme is that of demonstrated success. The message from the first is "We know where we are going, and we know how to get there!" The message from the second is "Look how far we've come already. Come on and join us, because we're going to make it!"

6: Turning Points in the Organizational Life Cycle

> People, products, markets, even societies, have life-cycles—
> birth, growth, maturity, old age, and death. At every life-cycle
> passage a typical pattern of behavior emerges . . . As the or-
> ganization passes from one phase of its life to the next, different
> roles are emphasized and the different role combinations that
> result produce different organizational behavior . . . The [life-
> cycle] model enables an organization to foresee the problems it
> will face as it grows over time. Furthermore, it . . . presents a
> framework for prescribing the treatments most likely to be ef-
> fective depending on the life-cycle stage of the organization.
>
> Ichak Adizes, "Organizational Passages"*

The idea that organizations and societies have life cycles has been
around for a long time. Europe is the Old World and America the
New World, and we mean by that more than that many of our
families used to live there before they came here. When we say that
Apple is a younger company than IBM, we mean something more
than that it was founded more recently. We mean something about
its energy, its brash self-confidence, its idealism. We talk about the
"growing pains" of rapidly expanding companies, the "comfortable
middle age" of established firms, and the "over-the-hill gang" at
General Motors. We call the demise of W. T. Grant a "death," and
we wondered for a while if Bank of America was dying too. The
life-cycle image is a natural one.

The life cycle is more than an analogy, however, for it also provides an important way to understand the larger significance of a
particular transition. The ending that starts a transition may be
traumatic because it is not just a particular set of circumstances that
is finished but a whole chapter of the organization's life. The beginning is difficult because it is the start of a new organizational life

phase, rather than simply a new situation. It is transition's developmental function in the life cycle that makes it the profound upheaval that it is.

To understand transition in this context, we need a map of the organizational life cycle that is comparable to the map of the individual life cycle that developmental psychologists use. Without such a map and a concept like "adolescence," individual crises after puberty would seem to be only idiosyncratic difficulties. It is only with the help of the idea of "adolescence" and its place in human development that we can see what is really going on, and the same thing is true in the case of an organization. A picture of the organizational life cycle will also help us to understand the key issues that must be dealt with by organizational leaders if they are to move through the transition successfully at each new stage in the organization's life.*

Shakespeare wrote about the Seven Ages of Man. Here are seven comparable "ages" of organizational life:

1. *The Dream:* The time of imagining and planning by the founder or founders; the phase—long or short, as the case may be —in which everything is still in people's minds and on pieces of paper. This is the period in which people sit around in somebody's office or living room brainstorming and arguing. It is a time of endless meetings and great excitement. There may or may not be a demonstrably effective product at this point, but the organization itself is "in utero." The Dream comes to an end when . . .

2. *The Venture* begins. The Venture is the organization's infancy and childhood, when it is small and changing rapidly. It exists in the world, but it is not yet independent of outside support. Money is consumed at an alarming rate and the organization begins to grow, but it cannot yet stand on its own two feet. Key figures in the undertaking may have to keep old jobs elsewhere to support themselves during part of this phase. At the beginning of The Venture the organization may be no more than a letterhead and a couple of people moonlighting or living off their savings while they try to attract capital, but by the end of The Venture the organization is actually delivering its product or its service to

some customer and starting to demonstrate its feasibility as a full-fledged organization. Whatever is done during The Venture is likely to be done in the easiest way: no policies, no fixed procedures, no real structure. But as The Venture becomes established, the need for a new phase of organizational life becomes evident—which is . . .

3. *Getting Organized:* This is the coming-of-age point in the organizational life cycle; it is the point where the natural energy of the founders is no longer enough. The organization is no longer simply the frantic efforts of a handful of people; it must now be a more predictable set of actions by a growing number of people. This is the time when people's roles begin to become more specialized and more impersonally defined, when financial controls are established and refined, when employment policies are spelled out, and when the data is computerized and company publications begin to be more than money-raising documents. Presuming that Getting Organized works, the organization moves ahead into . . .

4. *Making It:* Now the organization is beginning to reap the rewards of its successful development in the form of increases in size, new products, reputation in the market, and rising profits. It has a solid foothold in the market, and while it may still be facing serious competition, it is established and can look forward to the prospect of further success. Making It can last for decades and can encompass many subchapters of growth, crisis, reorganization, and reorientation. It is less easy to describe Making It as a phase in itself than as a phase that comes after the point when the basic systems are fully in place and before . . .

5. *Becoming an Institution:* The shift here is subtle but profound: from doing to being, from external results to internal style, from staking out territory to occupying it. People's energy begins to be taken up with how things ought to be done and what is appropriate to an organization like this one. New people are chosen less for their talent or motivation than for how they will fit in with "us." Reputation is now a given, not something being earned, and people may forget that until very recently they were struggling to

establish themselves. There is a timeless quality to this phase, a sense of having arrived and a loss of urgency about moving on. Like the previous phase, this one can last a long time and can be punctuated by changes in leadership, acquisitions and divestitures, and subtle changes in priority or direction. IBM and the old AT&T were well-established "institutions" for a long time. IBM still is, and AT&T is trying to cycle back into a new form of Making It. Unless something is consciously done to prevent it, most institutions move beyond this fifth phase of organizational life and begin . . .

6. *Closing In:* In some cases, this phase grows almost imperceptibly out of the self-satisfaction of the previous one, and when there is continued success and not too much competition from outside, the inward turning may produce a rather attractive "aristocratic" stylization of effort. When the organization is a governmental body that does not need to demonstrate success in the marketplace, the result is more likely to be an increasingly unresponsive bureaucracy. But if the market is competitive, the result is far less satisfactory; the organization turns inward in a way that sometimes seems perverse, so that people argue about rules and statuses while the whole operation is slowly collapsing. (An executive in a bank where this is going on calls it "Fighting over deck chairs on the *Titanic.*") Whatever the external situation and however quickly the organization is undermined by it, the Closing In breaks the vital tension between the organization and its environment. Although it can be kept alive for some time by extraordinary assets or a monopolistic position, the natural and final outcome of Closing In is . . .

7. *Termination:* Unlike individuals who can be pronounced dead at a particular time, organizations more often disappear than die. They get acquired or split up. Their functions are changed, and then their names are changed, and then their assets are sold. They vanish into bankruptcy proceedings and operate with skeleton staffs in tiny offices somewhere over a warehouse. But the fact remains—sooner or later the activities and the identity that were that organization no longer exist, and the life cycle of that organization is terminated.

In the context of this seven-stage life cycle, transitions are the dynamic interlude between one life stage and the next. A single transition may not accomplish the complete transformation of the organization, however, and so there may be a cluster of transitions or an extended string of transitions, each of which carries the organization another step along the way from The Venture to Getting Organized or from Making It to Becoming an Institution. Each transition ends some aspect of the old phase and begins some aspect of the new. Such multitransition turnings may take years. However long they take, it is only as parts of these developmental transformations that we can fully understand what transitions accomplish in an organization.

Even the emergence of The Dream in the first place is a transition for the people involved, for there is always some existing status quo for which The Dream offers a replacement. Thus, no matter how much promise it holds, The Dream is likely to be experienced by those identified with existing institutions as a threat.

Minimills, which reprocess scrap into new steel, began as such a dream. The existing steel companies held fast to the more expensive and burdensome process of making the metal out of ore. The Dream survived and grew, although it could do so only outside the existing organizations. The same thing happened with The Dream of using transistors instead of vacuum tubes in radios, computers, and other electronic instruments. Again, the big American companies that were successfully using vacuum tubes refused to embrace the new technology, and left that Dream to the Japanese to nurture.

The Dream is always the enemy of the status quo, and that is why the champions of the new are so often peripheral to the old. The transition to The Dream is very difficult for people whose identity is tied up with the way things are presently being done, and anyone who has ever tried to explain a really new and exciting idea to partisans of the old will recall that despite all the apparent open-mindedness, they viewed The Dream as at best impractical, and at worst subversive.

The Dreamer is likely to feel superior to those who oppose him, to call the people who cannot make the transition to embrace The Dream "reactionaries," and to dismiss them as different from people who are willing to change and grow. But in a little while the

Dreamer will have a transition to make, too. The Dream stage of the life cycle, when everyone talks excitedly about "what we'll do" and "how things will be" is the happiest time in the organization's history for some Dreamers. The idea is pure—no compromises yet, no dilution, no blunders. Even though the organization does not yet really exist in external form, some Dreamers can become so enamored of this first stage of the organization's life that they refuse to leave it. These are the people who have great ideas but don't do anything with them. They may even have a string of great ideas and live with the frustration of seeing someone else pick them up and develop them into something.

The organizational world is full of such Dreamers. The transition that they have difficulty making involves letting go of the perfect ideal or the effortless vision and coming to terms with the reality of hard work and compromise. Some who do let themselves go into the transition at the end of The Dream fail ever fully to emerge from it, but are instead carried unwillingly forward while they reminisce about the old days "when we sat around Charlie's kitchen table and talked about the new kind of school [or store, or factory] that we'd start." They are wholly committed to The Dream, but they find a dozen reasons why the moment isn't quite right to turn it into a real Venture. If others push forward in spite of them, they manage in subtle ways to impede every step ahead because it is a step away from The Dream.

Not everyone finds the transition from The Dream to The Venture so difficult, of course, for some people are not so interested in The Dream itself as in creating an actual undertaking based upon it. They are the people who do not feel really comfortable until there is an office and a phone, an ad in the paper and an actual service or product that is deliverable to a real customer.

Even at this early point in the organizational life cycle, the First Law of Organizational Growth is evident: Those who were most at home with the necessary activities of one developmental stage are most likely to experience the next stage as a loss. Just as the Dreamers can worry and even grow bitter about the activities that The Venture needs if it is to succeed, so champions of The Venture can find the transition to Getting Organized very difficult.

The Venture is exemplified by Hewlett-Packard in the late thirties, Apple Computer in the early eighties, and thousands of lesser endeavors between. It does just fine for a while in someone's garage or spare bedroom, and when it outgrows that space it is likely to move into a larger version of a garage or a spare room rather than into fancy new quarters. Typically, the organization is run by its founder or founders and a handful of people who are caught up in the founder's enthusiasm. Roles are vague, and well-articulated policies are nonexistent. The only requirement is to get problems solved as they present themselves, and the worst mistake is to miss an opportunity.

The Venture demands entrepreneurial hustle. How things are done does not matter much, for in the crisis-driven atmospheres of most Ventures, energy, a pragmatic and flexible approach, commitment, and the ability to interest others in the undertaking are more important than elaborate plans and systems. There is very little formal hierarchy, although there is seldom any doubt who has the ultimate power. The values are those of the founder, and his or her personality defines the style of the whole organization. No formal decision-making process exists. The founder decides or tells someone else to decide. The people who cluster around such founders tend to be comfortable with someone else calling the shots, and they are likely to admire and idealize the founders. Loyalty is personal.

A Venture can last a long time, as further funding is needed for the next expansion . . . and the next. The people who are at home in this world can be so well adjusted to it that they are threatened by its very success. For success generates more complex situations and more data than the undefined roles and the seat-of-the-pants tactics can handle. The success of The Venture initiates the transition to the next phase, that of Getting Organized. And thus we come to the Second Law of Organizational Growth: The successful outcome of any phase of the organizational life cycle triggers its demise.

This sequence of Dream-to-Venture-to-Organization characterizes the earliest days of everything from Standard Oil to Celestial Seasonings. It is the pattern followed by manufacturing companies and service organizations. In a recent seminar that I conducted, the minister of a rapidly growing Southern California church found that it fitted her organization's history, as did the president of a temporary employment agency and the vice-president in charge of a new and semi-autonomous data-processing division of a large bank. It is easiest to study in rapidly developing high-tech companies, however, because in such organizations the phases follow one another relatively quickly and the transitions are more clearly defined than they are with slower-moving organizations.

Biocorp, Inc., is not a real name, but I want to preserve a real company's anonymity because the problems it is having with transition are so typical that it would be unfair to burden its fragile hold on existence by calling public attention to it in that way. Located in one of those clusters of university spin-offs outside a large eastern city, Biocorp was founded six years ago to develop a biologist's pioneering genetic research into marketable products.

The founder was a maverick at the university who had gathered around him a handful of devoted graduate students who were more interested in his ideas than in their own degrees. The founder pursued his dream in the university's laboratories as long as he could, and then with $75,000 from a mortgage on his house, he set up a lab in an old building not far from the campus. Some of his graduate students gladly joined him, and The Venture began.

From the beginning, the founder's group was polarized into the Dreamers and the Venturers, and the two groups struggled to gain his approval and blessing. The founder managed to stay neutral, however, somehow honoring both the pristine dream and the enthusiasm of the doers. No one had any employment agreement or benefits. Everyone worked for minimum wage, and the prospect of owning a small part of a great new company. Decisions on research strategy were nominally made by consensus, although the founder could almost always convince the others to do what he believed they ought to. There was no formal budget, and the founder's own checking account statements were the closest thing the company had to financial records. Supplies and equipment were bought piecemeal and kept in a bookcase. Inventory procedures did not exist, because there was so little to inventory.

The founder conducted The Venture's external relations in the same haphazard fashion. He spoke at professional meetings, he visited people that former colleagues told him invested in start-up companies, and he gave a Xeroxed prospectus on his as-yet-nonexistent product line to anyone who expressed an interest. But he did manage to attract the attention of a venture capitalist, who was impressed by what he believed the founder could do, put together a group of investors, and raised $13 million to get a decent research and manufacturing site, to hire production workers, and (he insisted on this) to bring in several people with managerial experience to get things organized. Biocorp, Inc., was in transition.

When I arrived a year later, the company was in chaos. The new managers had set up formal budgeting and accounting procedures, spelled out conditions of employment for everyone, set up functional departments with well defined responsibilities, and done the other things that a rapidly growing company requires to run effectively. All the systems were in place to turn a Venture into an Organization, but they had completely disregarded the transitions that the changes had created. Most of what made the original core of employees valuable to The Venture made them detrimental to the Organization. The founder himself, with his disorganized creativity and his charismatic hold on his little circle of research assistants, was constantly blocking plans to bring out a commercially viable product. His intuitive way of following opportunities as they arose, which had guided his research and found him the venture capital he needed, was now a handicap in a situation that required systematic planning.

The early history of Biocorp, Inc., illustrates the Third Law of Organizational Growth: In any significant transition you are forced to give up the very thing that got you that far. Growth, the thing that everyone desires, requires relinquishment. The owner of a small California winery that has recently won several big prizes put the matter simply: "We're at 10,000 cases a year now and still precarious financially. We could go to 15,000, maybe 20,000 pretty quickly, and from a business point of view we should. But at every step you lose something—some personal control of quality, some employee willingness to go the 'extra mile,' some direct involvement with the whole process that made it worth it to work for fourteen hours a day!"

Sometimes, however, a founder has enough personal need for structure so that Getting Organized is not such a painful process. In that case, the founder champions the new functional role definitions, the new information management system, the new financial controls. It is not until the organization is poised on the edge of the next transition into Making It that the founder pulls back and begins to undermine the efforts to move from a promising new company to one that has a foothold in its market. An example of a transition that has been aborted in this way is provided by Energy Conversion Devices, Inc., a company founded and run by Stanford R. Ovshinsky, the man that *Business Week* called the "messianic guru of so-called amorphous materials."*

Ovshinsky attracted more than $200 million in development funds from such industrial heavyweights as Arco, Canon, Nippon Steel, and Standard Oil. Armed with 226 patents on devices involving new kinds of solar cells, optical memories, and special magnets, Ovshinsky's company has spent almost two decades on the verge of great breakthroughs. Time and again he announced that a whole new day for electronic devices was at hand, and each time the day has failed to dawn.

No one doubts the importance of the basic ideas Ovshinsky is working with, but he is clearly more interested in working with the ideas than he is in the systematic efforts to turn them into products. A reporter who studied his operations noted that he "frequently diverts resources to new research projects at the expense of developing marketing expertise and moving products into the marketplace." He stays afloat by continuing to attract investors with his brilliant promise and by "surrounding himself only with loyal subordinates." As I write this, his board is putting pressure on him to make the transition that he is avoiding, and his investors are attaching more and more strings to the funds they give him. But he has shown no signs of changing his ways or bringing in someone else who is ready to make the transition to Making It. Ovshinsky certainly wants his company to prosper and he probably wants it to increase in size, but in the terms we are using here he does not want it to *grow*. He is like the parent who is devoted to his child but unable to see that it is time to let the child grow up.

Apple is the opposite case. Its CEO, John Scully, has not just put the company back on its feet after a season of troubles. He has taken an organization that his predecessor had kept trying to turn back into a bigger and better Venture, and has brought it through a critical transition into the phase of Making It. The problems that Scully faced when he arrived—the first quarterly loss in Apple's history as a public company, a 20 percent layoff, and Steve Jobs's difficult ouster—were not just isolated problems to be solved, but signs of the end of a phase of organizational life.

What Scully has demonstrated is that organizational growth is qualitative as well as quantitative, and it involves a sequence of different phases, just as the growth of a human being involves the very distinct phases of infancy, childhood, adolescence, and so on. His situation illustrates the Fourth Law of Organizational Development, which is that whenever there is a painful time of troubles, a developmental transition is probably at hand. It also illustrates the Fifth Law, which is that up through the life phase of Becoming an Institution, *not* making a transition when the time is at hand creates a state of "developmental retardation" in which physical expansion may continue for a time, but real growth is aborted and in the end the organization's very life is threatened.

Apple is Making It today, as it was not two years ago. It remains to be seen, however, whether it will continue to develop over the years and become an Institution. The question is not whether its leaders will grow fat and self-satisfied, but only whether the challenges that go with becoming part of the established order will replace those of breaking into the established order. The challenges will not disappear, nor will the changes necessary to meet them. Whatever happens in the years ahead, the success Apple has in Making It will begin to change the very challenges it faces.

"Institutions" are more than simply large organizations or old ones. They are the organizations that are established, the ones that control major sectors of the market, the ones whose policies help to define what a career in a particular field represents. Some, like Johnson & Johnson and 3M, are known for innovativeness, though most are less innovative than smaller and younger companies. Some, like Delta Airlines and Hewlett-Packard have reputations as organizations that are very much concerned with the well-being of their employees, but many of the companies that make the lists of the "best companies to work for" are not yet full-fledged Institutions. Their common element and what sets them apart from organizations at other stages of the life cycle is that they have a staff,

financial resources, planning and managing capabilities, and production facilities that are "mature." Boeing, Procter & Gamble,
Westinghouse, Exxon—all are Institutions.

Less mature organizations may be very large and very successful,
but like young employees there is still a "provisional" quality about
their accomplishments and their positions. Like young employees,
they are still trying to prove themselves, still (under the confident
surface) a little unsure where they belong in the order of things.
They are, like young individuals, still motivated by notions of their
own uniqueness and invulnerability that are untested by time. There
is a confidence in the young organization that is both attractive and
dangerous, exciting and unrealistic.

There are costs to Becoming an Institution, however. For one
thing, form begins to be more important than function. Communications cease to be the way to get through to others and begins to
become a demonstration of acceptable style. People grow less likely
to communicate directly with those that need to know and more
likely to "go through channels." Efforts that involve doing things
differently are paced slowly in the name of "bringing everyone on
board." In the end it often turns out, as it did at a large manufacturing facility where I consulted, that so many compromises have to be
made to guarantee everyone's support that the effort to change is
dissipated. Institutions are so concerned with the stability of their
own internal systems and the sanctity of their cultural values that in
the end they are likely to generate the kinds of crises that initiate
the transition to the next phase of the organizational life cycle,
Closing In.

Institutionality is something like mid-life in the individual life
cycle. It is likely to be the time of greatest achievement in any
measurable sense, but it is also the time when a strange hollowness
begins to be felt: "What now?" "The excitement is gone." "Is this
all there is?" And as with individuals at mid-life, institutions are
likely to be challenged by circumstances to decide which of two
paths to follow henceforth.

The path of least resistance carries them toward an end that is as
organizationally natural as it may be unfortunate for all the people
involved. Institutions are already more introverted than the same
organizations were at the earlier stage of Making It, and as that

inwardness grows more pronounced a series of crises are likely to develop. Typically, the crises that bring Institutionality to an end and lead into the transition to Closing In are external threats to market position or funding. The Institutional concern for rules and policy is turned into an obsession with demonstrating that everything has been done properly and that the expectation of other results is itself improper. The existing concern for channels turns the organization into a warren of organizational tunnels into which requests disappear and from which results never emerge.

Much that goes under the name of *bureaucracy* comes from this Closing In. It is a mistake to treat bureaucracy as the natural post-Institutional phase of the organizational life cycle, however, since there are "bureaucratic" elements in the organization at all points in its history after it gets organized. The key characteristics of Closing In are not just that routine squeezes out all imagination and efficiency. It is that the organization seals itself off from effective communication with its environment and that it becomes preoccupied with its own inner workings to the point where they are ritualized into secret and magical acts.

Closed In organizations reject signals from outside as though they were irrelevant or even hostile. The peacetime Army and Navy are always somewhat Closed In organizations that turn back into Ventures in time of war and usually develop to the point of Making It during wartime. So military examples of how Closed In organizations behave are easy to find. One such example is the case of Continuous Aim Firing.*

At the end of the Spanish-American War an American naval officer named Sims discovered that the English had developed a way to compensate for the roll of a ship and to hold steady the barrel of a shipboard cannon that would otherwise be tilting up and down with the action of the waves. He showed that the English, using the new system, were dozens of times more accurate than American crews then were. He showed too that instead of having to time the firing to moments or relative stability between rolls, gunners could now aim and fire continuously.

He sent off his findings to the Bureau of Ordinance and the Bureau of Navigation, and he waited. And waited. It was only after he began circulating his reports through unofficial channels, in a manner that his superiors found little short of unethical, that he elicited a reply. Which was essentially this:

1. That our equipment was as good as that of the British, so the difference must be in the training of the gunners.

2. That the training of the gunner was not the responsibility of the bureaus in question but of the officers of particular ships.

3. And, most important, that "continuous-aim firing is impossible."

A footnote to the story is that Sims succeeded in breaking through this evasion and denial only by communicating directly with President Theodore Roosevelt. He recalled Sims from unofficial exile in China and appointed him Inspector of Target Practice, a post in which he could put his ideas into action. The historian Elting Morison described the results. In a test conducted three years before Sims took over his new gunnery post,

> . . . five ships of the North Atlantic Squadron fired five minutes each at a lightship hulk at the conventional range of 1600 yards. After twenty-five minutes of banging away, two hits had been made on the sails of the elderly vessel. Six years later [and after three years of Sims's work] one naval gunner made 15 hits in one minute at a target 75 × 25 feet at the same range; half of them hit in a bull's eye 50 inches square.

This is more than an example of technical innovation and an organization's resistance to it. It is an example of the natural behavior of the Closed In stage of the organizational life cycle and what one leader did to break it open again. We shall return to the subject of such efforts at organizational rejuvenation in a moment. But first we need to say a few words about the last organizational life phase, Termination.

Unlike people, organizations have neither natural life expectancies nor upper limits to their lifetimes. They are not mortal, and because there is no biological clock measuring their days it is easy to regard their deaths, when they occur, as unnatural. Yet to do so is a mistake, for although some deaths are self-inflicted and others are the result of mishap or mayhem, many organizations grow old and die as surely as people do. And many more organizations would do so if people could face the need for endings more squarely or, in the case of giant corporations in trouble, if Washington were not afraid of the repercussions when a Lockheed, a Chrysler, or a Continental Illinois collapsed.

A company dies when it is bought by another company and swallowed up by its new owner. A government department dies when its appropriations are cut out of the new budget, and a nonprofit agency dies when donations or grants stop. A little college can die when its enrollment falls below the break-even point, and a huge corporation can die when foreign competition drives it into bankruptcy.

In most cases, these deaths are more timely than anyone connected with the organization will admit. For the death of an organization isn't a mechanical failure, like a ship that sinks or a plane that crashes. It is an organic failure, more like the fall of a great oak in a storm. It comes from the same force of growth that in an earlier day caused expansion and maturity. Termination is usually as natural to its place in the organizational life cycle as is The Venture or Making It are natural to their places. To lead an organization through a Termination with care and dignity is as important an organizational task as it is to it through Getting Organized or Becoming an Institution. And managing a Termination well takes as much skill as managing any other phase of the life cycle.

In spite of the naturalness of organizational aging and the timeliness of many Terminations, it is also true that an organization does not have to die. We noted earlier that up to the stage of Becoming an Institution, an organization that does not move on to the next stage aborts its natural growth. But once Institutionality is reached, organizations no longer follow the same law. Like people at mid-life they have a choice of three paths: those of Denial, Formalism, and Rejuvenation.

The path of Denial usually begins with the proclamation that the organization is as strong and vital as it ever was. It is the quickest path through Closing In and toward Termination, for it denies the existence of the very signals from outside that might restore a vital connection between the organization and its environment. When an Institution begins to follow the path of Denial, it cultivates the party line and weeds out its critics, staking its hopes on its reputation and the tried-and-true systems it has developed. It Closes In and decays quickly, finally dying like W. T. Grant, being swallowed up like Eastern Airlines, or being artificially sustained by bankruptcy support systems like LTV Corp.

The path of Formalism ends up the same way, although it takes longer to get there. It involves a flurry of restructuring, some selling of old businesses and acquiring new ones to refocus the organization's energies on "our core businesses," and an effort to redefine and strengthen the organization's traditional culture. Although these efforts produce a temporary sense of recovered purpose and an improved balance sheet—and may even expand the organization in the short run—they are really ways of warding off contact with everything in the future that is unfamiliar and risky. In so doing, organizations on the path of Formalism insulate themselves from revitalization and head down the path toward Closing In and Termination.

At present, Goodyear Tire & Rubber Co. seems to be taking this path, as does Owens-Corning. It is worth noting that both did so to avoid takeover threats. Only time will tell, but I very much doubt the common argument that the threat of takeovers makes management do its job by making it tighten up the organization. In fact, the belt tightening takes all the slack out of the system so that the price of risk taking becomes too high and Closing In accelerates.

The path of Rejuvenation is, as the name suggests, a return to the youthfulness that characterized earlier phases in the organizational life cycle. It has been described by other names in the current spate of books on Excellence, Innovation, and Productivity.* That is why I am not devoting more space to its details here, for my concern is to show that Rejuvenation is not just a set of strategies for managers and leaders to follow in all organizations but is, rather, an opportunity to recover youthfulness in a mature organization. It is a strategy that a younger organization would not need, but it is also one which a younger organization would lack the maturity to capitalize upon.

Rejuvenation, which may involve some particular project, a division of a large organization, or a whole Institution as such, essentially recapitulates the whole cycle of organizational growth. It begins with new or newly articulated Dreams, one or more Ventures which evolve their own structures in the process of Getting Organized. Rejuvenation finally achieves the vital effectiveness of Making It, but it does so by beginning over again rather than by trying to inject vitality and effectiveness into an aging organization.

Organizations that are undertaking this Institutional path toward Rejuvenation include Campbell Soup, which has been broken up into fifty independent business units—each a Venture, with a charter to develop its own products. Countless hospitals in America that are launching satellite chemical dependency programs, sports medicine clinics, occupational therapy centers, and women's health clinics also are attempting to follow the path of Rejuvenation. G.E. and Dow Chemical are doing the same thing. In these companies Jack Welch and Paul Orrefice have launched complete Rejuvenation programs that aim to replace "aging" units with "younger" ones.*

By the time an organization becomes institutionalized, it is likely to be so complex that it is really more like a family than like a single individual. Different parts of an Institution are likely to be at different life stages. While that represents a management challenge, it is also a source of vitality, for over time a planned series of transitions of people and assets from aging parts of the organizational "family" to the younger parts can be effected. This effort requires good strategic planning, a well-coordinated reorganization scheme, and tactics for dealing with the transitions that everyone will have to go through.

As separate strategies, planning and reorganizing are too familiar to require either description or prescription here. But their developmental function is less often appreciated. Because of the transitions that they produce, planning and reorganization are likely to be no more than unprofitable disruptions of normal activity if their developmental function is not maximized and called to people's attention. While there are a number of points in the life cycle of an organization where growth is promoted by planning and reorganization, the point of Institutional Rejuvenation is clearly the most important in today's socioeconomic situation, where mature and relatively inflexible American organizations are losing out to younger and more vital foreign competitors.

Although all transitions force individuals and organizations to let go of some of the qualities and strategies that got them this far, an organization's challenge in the Institutional phase of its life is particularly difficult because it requires reversing the whole direction of its development up to that point. So far, everything that led to growth required moving away from the amorphous energy of organizational youth. But now there must be a recovery of that energy and youth if vitality is to be maintained.

Yet this Rejuvenation must be more than a middle-aged longing for the excitement of a lost youth, for the wisdom that is the gift of age is the other half of what Rejuvenation requires. The mid-life analogy is useful, for as Daniel Levinson has pointed out, "A major developmental task of the Mid-life Transition is to . . . seek new ways of being Young [and] Old [at the same time]."* People who can do that can tap into the sources of vitality that are natural to middle age and avoid the pitfalls of either going "over the hill" or trying to deny aging with a sad counterfeit of youthfulness.

Organizations that can do that are both vital and mature. The recent rapacious acquisitiveness of the Allegheny Corporation suggests what it looks like for an organization to deny its real age. USX and GM, on the other hand, suggest what it looks like to lose touch with the capacity for inner youthfulness and slide slowly toward an unhappy old age.

In closing this discussion of the typical phases of organizational growth, I want to note that the Seven Ages of Organizational Life seldom look as clear to the participants as they do to the observer who studies the organization after the fact. One reason for this has already been discussed: All organizational settings are enormously complicated by the presence of different levels of development. There are also two other reasons: (1) There is always old and unfinished developmental business within the organization, and (2) There is difficulty in perceiving the movement from one stage to the next when it is broken up into several apparently unrelated transitions.

I spoke earlier of the organizational tendency toward "retarded development." It is almost universal. Old problems are not quite solved, but instead are temporarily buried. In one company where I have consulted, the old problems are those of power within the conglomerate "family"—specifically the inability of the youthful Ventures to gain the autonomy they need to be fully effective. The company that I worked with was Making It, but in every transition its developmental issues were obscured by the old question of how much authority the parent was going to grant the child.

Another of my clients, a large manufacturing facility that was trying to rejuvenate itself, found that in the process of getting organized, it had never created an effective human resources department. In its place it had an old-style personnel office, where labor relations and employment records were the main concern. Training and organizational development capabilities of the sort required for a major Rejuvenation effort simply didn't exist. The failure to deal adequately with Getting Organized would always emerge to handicap the company at later points of developmental transition. Like the middle-aged man still tied to his mother's apron strings, the organization had failed to accomplish a developmental task in its rightful season.

The second reason that developmental issues are often unclear in a transitional situation is that transitions, which are huge from the point of view of the people affected, may represent very small steps in the organization's growth. Take the case of MCI, for example.* As its founder, Bill McGowan, has recently retold it, the story of MCI was the story of being in a whole series of different businesses. To begin with, he told an interviewer, "Everybody said, 'Oh, you're going into microwave communications, [the original company name was Microwave Communications] but that was not true at all. The business I was going into was *raising venture capital.*" That was a Venture activity if there ever was one—as was the "next business we got into, which was *lobbying the United States government*" to let MCI provide long-distance service in competition with AT&T.

The next business McGowan found himself in was *"actually building a long-distance network,*" and after that, when AT&T decided to block access to local customers through its lines, "our business shifted once again—to *winning lawsuits and simply surviving.*" Once the suits had been won and other companies began crowding in to capitalize on the opportunity, McGowan realized that only the biggest ones could survive, so "the thrust of our [next business] was *to grow—and grow as fast as we could.*" It was only after that point that MCI could make the transition to the "business" that it had nominally been in all along: *providing good long-distance service for its customers.* By that point MCI was no longer a

Venture, but was dealing with the central issues of Making It. The route it took to get there had been punctuated by wrenching transitions, each of which developed The Venture and helped it to get organized.

The crises of MCI's ongoing operations often made it difficult to see the development that was going on, but in an apparently meandering set of steps the company grew and matured. Just as with an individual, the stages are buried under a mass of confusing details. But, as with the individual, it is the progression of stages and not the sum of the details that tells us how the organization has really changed.

When I first began working with organizations in transition, I dreamed of working out a model of the organizational life cycle so sophisticated that one could match any situation against it and say, "There we are!" I have failed to be so precise, for life-cycle models are a little like one-size-fits-all clothes, which is to say that they fit no one very exactly. What they do, however, is to provide occasional but important glimpses through the *what* of organizational transition into the *why*.

Our present model of the organizational life cycle is accurate enough in most cases to suggest why it is time to let go of the dreaming that was so exciting and get down to the hard work of making a project fly. Then to make it clear why it is time to let go of chasing down opportunities and take time to get policies and procedures clear. And after that to demonstrate why it is time to leave that organizational effort behind and get on with the task of carving out a piece of the market. Then to show why it is time to turn back inward again and mature the enterprise into a full-scale Institution. And then why at that point the critical transitions will confront the organization with the decision of whether to Close In further or cycle back toward a new birth in a project of organizational Rejuvenation.

Without the context of organizational growth, the transitions will be full of pain and promise, but they do not finally mean anything more than getting from one situation to another. But with the meaning that the developmental context provides, transitions can be seen not as random events but as steps in a sequence that makes sense. That context is very important, because meaningful transitions can be managed, while meaningless crises can only be survived.

7: Leadership and Transition

If the blind lead the blind, both shall fall into the ditch.
The Gospel According to Matthew 15:14

No one doubts the importance of leadership, but many descriptions of what it entails are so general that they offer little help in distinguishing good leadership from bad. Other descriptions are so specific that they limit the idea of leadership to some specific kind of leader, denying the title to people who have undoubtedly guided organizations or groups through difficult situations. Still other descriptions are so cryptic that they stimulate the imagination but offer little guidance to someone who is trying to make actual leadership decisions that affect the long-term well-being of an organization. Studies of individual leaders, convincing when viewed singly, can be quite confusing in their diversity when taken as a group.

Recognizing that there are different kinds of leaders is a first step to clearing up this confusion. James MacGregor Burns's distinction between Transactional and Transformational leaders is a good starting point.* In some situations, he points out, the leader has done the job if he or she has set the immediate priorities in terms of some existing purpose and has allocated the resources accordingly—in the Transactional manner. But when the organization's objectives and values are no longer adequate to its situation, something more is demanded. A Transformational leader is called for, one who can redefine the organization's purpose and rebuild its resources to deal with the challenge that it faces.

Steve Jobs was clearly a Transformational leader at Apple, but so in another sense is his successor, John Scully. The "transformations" differed, but both were far-reaching. Jobs transformed a Dream into one of the most successful Ventures in the history of American business, while Scully transformed the Venture into an

organization that is going to Make It over the long pull. Scully is
not just a caretaker of his predecessor's successes, but a man who is
leading Apple through the next transition that it needed to make in
order to grow.

The categories of Transformation and Transaction tell us less
about leaders than they do about our cultural penchant for polariz-
ing people into the good guys who want to change things and the
bad guys (or at least, the less good ones) who want to keep them the
way they are. It would be more useful to say that it takes some kind
of Transformative approach to initiate any new phase of the organizational life cycle, but that the very same leaders who provide that
initiative in the beginning will probably end up being Transactional
once they get things going their way. Revolutionaries become conservative once they have their own status quo to protect. We need
something more than Burns's two categories—something closer to
the actual diversity of leadership styles and the way the different
styles fit different phases of the growth cycle. Perhaps if we start
with actual examples, we'll do better.

When people say "leader," they think of people like Napoleon or
Joan of Arc, Iacocca or Lincoln. They think of figures that draw
followers to them by a magnetism that amazes and sometimes dis-
mays others. Such leaders are people who can stake their whole
future on a possibility that they believe in, and they have an intuitive feel for social and psychological possibilities that often mystify
more matter-of-fact types. These possibilities are sometimes a little
vague in their detail, but as depicted by such leaders they are compelling to many followers. It is this kind of "vision" of what could
be that such leaders use to rally others to action, and it is often the
critical factor in saving an organization or even a whole society in a
time of turmoil and danger.

Winston Churchill was such a leader. "We shall go on to the
end," he said during the lowest ebb of Britain's wartime fortunes.
"We shall fight in France, we shall fight on the seas and oceans, we
shall fight with growing confidence and growing strength in the air,
we shall defend our island, whatever the cost may be, we shall fight
on the beaches, we shall fight on the landing grounds, we shall fight
in the fields and in the streets, we shall fight in the hills; we shall
never surrender."

Churchill's natural approach to the world was to relate the situation he was facing to people's feelings rather than to their thinking. This is not to say that Churchill was not a profoundly intellectual man, for his historical writings make it clear that he was. It is only to say that when he sought to capture the attention of his followers and to persuade them of something, he appealed to their hearts rather than their heads and to their personal associations rather than to their impersonal understandings. It is typical that when he formed his first wartime government, he offered the House of Commons a personal commitment rather than a public program: "I would say to the House, as I said to those who have joined this Government, 'I have nothing to offer but blood, toil, tears and sweat.' "

Like other leaders of his type Churchill was very articulate and had a metaphorical turn of mind. He coined the term "iron curtain." His epigrams have found their way into books of quotations: "The inherent vice of capitalism is the unequal sharing of blessings; the inherent virtue of socialism is the equal sharing of miseries." He called democracy "the worst form of Government except all those other forms that have been tried from time to time." His wit skewered more than one opponent—as when he called Viscount Montgomery "in defeat, unbeatable; in victory, unbearable."

Churchill's type of leadership can be very effective in young organizations. Although organizational leaders must be more concerned about a product or a service than their political counterparts, they often draw people along after them with a similar kind of vision, which emphasizes social possibility. A profile of People Express founder Donald Burr recently traced the company's astounding rise from 250 to 4,000 employees and from three to sixty-nine jets—and $1 billion in revenue—in just four years.* That kind of growth occurs occasionally in the most successful high-tech companies, but it is unknown in the airline industry. And the allegiance that Burr generated among employees was a large part of his success. That allegiance, however, was not so much the effects of the low prices as from a person-oriented style of management. In Burr's words, "You don't just want to make a buck. You want people to become better people."

But the article from which that quote is taken was called "Bitter

Victories," and its main point is that after astounding early successes, Burr was beginning to have trouble at People Express. (Since the article was written, of course, that difficulty has turned into disaster and People Express has been sold to Texas Air.) With new kinds of competition from the established industry leaders, things had become much more difficult for Burr.

Burr said he struggled not to become bitter and not to let what he called "the bad forces" make him abandon his original vision in favor of more conventional systems and procedures. But the talk about "the bad forces" suggests that his vision had already been compromised by an antagonistic suspiciousness toward people whose motives are "lower" and more conventional than he asked of his employees. In this he illustrates one of the weaknesses of Churchillian types of leader, who find it hard not to take everything personally. Whenever they do, their idealism and focus on people can turn into a kind of paranoia.

That was true of Churchill too. When he came to look back on his years of wartime leadership, Churchill did not try to conceal his bitterness. In *The Gathering Storm,* he wrote:

> . . . on the night of the tenth of May [1940] at the outset of this mighty battle, I acquired the chief power in the State, which henceforth I wielded in ever-growing measure for five years and three months of world war, at the end of which time, all our enemies having surrendered unconditionally or being about to do so, I was immediately dismissed by the British electorate from all further conduct of their affairs.

But the issue was much more than merely personal. Behind the details of that election (which he lost) was a more general and quite impersonal issue that Churchill seems never to have grasped: The time for his kind of leadership was gone and another kind of leader was needed. The crisis that demanded total commitment was past, and in its wake was the enormous task of rebuilding and reorganizing a tired and badly battered country.

It is no accident that Churchill's successor, Clement Attlee, was a very different kind of leader. He was a lawyer who had been deeply influenced by the Socialist ideas of the Fabian Society at the turn of the century, when a Labour Government was just a reformer's dream. But Attlee himself was not a visionary in the sense that Churchill was. He was a careful builder, an adapter of others' ideas, an implementer, a man with a plan to remodel the entire socio-economic order of Great Britain. It is ironic that this practical and careful party man should have overseen far more changes than the dynamic Churchill ever dreamed of: the nationalization of iron and steel, of coal and gas and electricity, of the railways and the Bank of England; the enactment of extensive welfare legislation, including the National Health Service; and the granting of independence to the former colonies of India, Burma, and Pakistan.

The difference between them was not that Churchill was dynamic and Attlee static. Attlee was at least as ready as Churchill to lead his society through a time of deep and far-reaching change. But note what sort of change it was. It was the logical application of a collective plan, not the realization of a personal dream. He was just putting into practice what his party had been preparing to do for half a century—and doing it, moreover, with an enormous framework of regulations and commissions. It was, in fact, his complex system of economic controls that did him in six years later. By 1951 England's mood had shifted again, and Attlee's reliance on the immense new structure of laws and agencies was out of tune with the spirit of a society that no longer felt so precarious.

Churchill and Attlee represent a leadership pattern found in the history of many organizations—a charismatic leader pulling the organization through its time of troubles and then a careful successor rebuilding it piece by piece, as Harry Truman did after Franklin Roosevelt, Andrew Johnson tried to do after Lincoln, and Scully is doing after Jobs.

Both kinds of leaders bring about change, so both call on their followers to let go of their worlds and the identity that they had in them. Different kinds of followers are going to respond best to the different kinds of transition that these two leadership types are likely to face. Those who most readily respond to the visionary leaders are likely to think of themselves as the wave of the future, but let the time come for a transition involving consolidation and they begin to talk sadly about the old days when people were willing to take risks and when initiative wasn't hobbled by policies. ("Camelot is finished," is the phrase used by some of yesterday's "transformationalists" at Apple.) And the people who respond to the Attlee type of leader will grieve in just the same way when the time for consolidation passes and there is a transition to a new situation that demands someone who can rally people around a more passionate vision.

It is sometimes claimed that the selection of Popes has followed the principle of following an "outside man" with an "inside man"— which is a variation of the principle we have been talking about: first the extroverted leader who deals with the organization's relation to its environment; then the more introverted rebuilder who brings order to the confusion that the outside man is likely to have left behind.* However it may be in the Catholic Church, that pattern of alternation is common in organizations of all kinds, and it makes sense. There is no way to know just who will follow Iacocca at Chrysler, but it is unlikely to be another "Churchill."

While Iacoccas and Churchills are unlikely to succeed one another at the helm of an organization, there are sometimes strings of Attlees during a stable period in an organization's history. This is particularly likely to happen after the organization Becomes an Institution, for then the maintenance of "our way" becomes an end in itself, and strategies and priorities can survive relatively unchanged for several terms of leadership. These times of stasis give Attlees and Scullys an unmerited reputation for conservatism. But such leaders can lead a society or an organization through immense transitions. And, as one can see from Churchill's opposition to independence for former colonies, a visionary can hold on to the past as well as any reactionary.

These differences between these two kinds of leaders depend on very different, temperamentally based strategies that they naturally use to identify issues and make decisions. The Churchills of the world depend heavily on intuition and base their action on a broad-brush picture of the big issues that can make an Attlee look petty and bogged down by trivia. The Attlee type of leader, on the other hand, is someone with a detailed plan and a concern for the particulars of a situation that can make the first look careless, sloppy, and irresponsible by contrast. He or she will call the other type's appeal to intuition self-indulgent and deceptive, for the Attlees of the world insist that things make sense, that they work, that they be rational. The Churchills will reply that these practical leaders have no heart, cannot inspire people, and get lost in forests while counting the trees.

The debate between them rages on without any recognition that in its own time each style of leadership is quite appropriate and can save the organization. Leadership itself, thus, depends on a match between personal style and the developmental task being faced by the organization. Although there is no way to describe "a good leader," there are several different ways to describe leaders that are good at the various stages of a given organization's life cycle.

It takes more than a bipolar scheme to describe the key qualities of leadership, however. "Churchill" and "Attlee" are no better in that regard than are Transformational and Transactional, although they do have the advantage of not being so simplistically for and against change. There is a four-quadrant scheme that is much more useful, one that has evolved out of decades of research into psychological types using the most widely used instrument of its kind in the world, the Myers-Briggs Type Inventory.*

The MBTI, as it is called, is based on the work of the Swiss psychiatrist Carl Jung, who first suggested in the twenties that a great deal could be learned about people by determining their typical ways of perceiving and judging things. People tended, he discovered, to depend on either *intuition* or *sensation* for their perceptions —which is to say that they either looked at what something might become or what it presently was, at its emerging pattern or at its present details. Everyone, he said, had some of both tendencies and might respond differently in different situations, but each of us had a preference for either *intuition-* or *sensation*-based perception.

He found that each person also had a preferred style of judging or making decisions. Some people did those things more or less impersonally on the basis of general principles, and he called theirs the *thinking* style. Others did them on the basis of personal values, and he called theirs the *feeling* style. Everyone, thus, has a combination of perceiving and judging that falls into one of four categories: intuition-with-thinking, intuition-with-feeling, sensation-with-thinking, and sensation-with-feeling.

The results of the MBTI testing have been compared, culture with culture, profession with profession, education level with education level, and organizational status with organizational status. The results substantiate the point being made in this chapter—that different temperaments work best in different situations. No wonder that "good leaders" are not all of one type. Effective leadership can be exercised by very different kinds of people if they capitalize on their strengths, compensate for their weaknesses, and gravitate toward situations where their natural temperament gives them an advantage. There is no such thing as one set of qualities that deserve the title, "Leadership Qualities."

The leaders we have been calling Churchills perceive things intuitively and make their decisions on the basis of personal values (intuition-with-feeling), while the Attlees perceive things in a more sensate style and make their decisions on the basis of impersonal principle (sensation-with-thinking). For convenience, we will call the former type Catalyst leaders, because they often create new outcomes by their very presence in a situation. We will call the latter Structural leaders, for their gift is the ability to bring new form to chaotic situations.

The other two kinds of leaders—Conceptuals and Relationals—also sometimes find themselves in opposition within an organization. The Conceptual leaders, who use intuition-with-thinking, are the idea people of the organizational world, while the Relationals who use sensation-with-feeling, are the "people" people. The Relationals are always concerned with how everyone is feeling and whether they are working well together, while the Conceptuals are more concerned with whether goals are clear and whether systems are efficient. Let's take these two types one at a time.

Conceptuals have some similarities to Catalysts, for both of them are future-oriented. But because their decisions are based on thinking rather than feeling, a Conceptual's vision is more likely to involve expertise or technical excellence than is a Catalyst's. The latter's vision is more likely to deal with realizing the human potentialities in a situation than with solving technical problems. The Catalyst is strongly motivated to discover the deeper meanings of situations and is likely to assume (incorrectly) that all other types are equally on a quest for meaning. The Conceptual, on the other hand, is more strongly motivated to understand things and to be able to explain them—and to assume (wrongly) that everyone is similarly interested in those questions.

Relational leaders are like Structurals in being less responsive by nature to the great visions of the future than they are to questions of how the present might be improved. Both types notice problems in the present that Catalysts and Conceptuals would probably fail to notice or consider insignificant if they did, but Structurals and Relationals differ as to what they see or want to do about it. Structurals believe that if things were organized completely rationally, procedures were spelled out in full detail, and all the facts were in hand, everything would go perfectly. They notice any shortcomings in these areas and have a natural instinct for correcting them. Relationals, on the other hand, are not so concerned with "the facts"— and may even be bothered that anyone could take such lifeless things so seriously—but they are no less concerned with how things are organized. Their interest in that issue is different, however, for they favor well-organized situations because they help people to feel comfortable, to know where they stand, and to understand what is expected of them. That such situations are often very efficient is viewed by them as a side benefit.

As the name suggests, Relational leaders are very aware of how people "relate to" what an organization is and does, and how they "relate to" one another. Such leaders often play a critical role in putting the pieces back together again after some kind of a trauma has demoralized an organization or a whole society. Gerald Ford was a Relational leader and played that role after the Watergate debacle. To a lesser degree, Ronald Reagan stepped into that role after the national loss of face in the Iranian hostage stalemate. Like most Relational leaders, both men have been criticized for not understanding the complex issues that they faced, but both also managed to achieve practical results that their opponents, with their more thoughtful and critical styles, often failed to accomplish. And both impressed opponents, who were sometimes appalled by their ideas, with their personal warmth and decency.

In a service business a Relational Leader can be a very effective entrepreneur. Debbi Fields, of cookie fame, is such a leader.* "It's a people company," she has said. " 'Mrs. Fields' is in the business of selling cookies, but that's just what the customer believes. What we really do is . . . we take care of people." Like any good leader,

Fields does not let the sign that happens to be over the door define "the business" that she is in. She defines it herself.

Some food service operations, like competing David's Cookies, take the Structural approach. The CEO of that chain, David Liederman, believes that "you want to minimize the probability of error," which means either "minimizing the number of people involved or, when that is not practical, supervising them as closely as possible." Liederman quotes approvingly "a very close friend" who is Vice-President for Operations at The Horn & Hardart Co. When he asked him to define his job, the friend said, 'My job is to keep my employees stealing as little as possible.' Liederman used the story to illustrate what the leader must do.

Compare Fields's Relational approach:

> I believe people will do their very best, I really do, provided that they are getting proper support . . . Sometimes I've gone into a store, and we haven't had the soft-and-chewy-cookies [which are the Fields trademark] . . . I'll go in and throw away $600 worth of product. I don't think about what I'm throwing away . . . I just assume that there's been some reason why the people were not taught what the standards of the company are. So I'll say, "Okay, let me explain. These cookies are not perfect, and we have to have perfect cookies. That's the goal." I'll take a cookie from the sheet and I'll say, "Eat this one. Do you see that it's crunchy?" And they'll say, "Yes." I'll say, "We don't sell crunchy cookies. What we sell are fresh, warm, and wonderful cookies. So, let's remove these from the shelf and let's go make a batch . . ." I'm there to teach [the employees]. I'm their support system. We do it together, and we start feeling good about what we're doing."

It is easy to make fun of this kind of militant sweetness and its disregard for ideas. Liederman, not too surprisingly, finds Fields's style very distasteful. But her critics miss the valid and effective Relational style of leadership that underlies her words and actions. Such people fail to see that at those times in an organization's life cycle when it is building (or rebuilding) solidarity and establishing (or reestablishing) a close bond with its customers, it may do well to redefine its business as *taking care of people*. If it chooses to do that, a Relational leader is the right person to lead the organization through its necessary transitions.

Unlike the Conceptual or the Catalyst, the Relational Leader is sensitive enough to practical issues to know when he or she needs help from people with a very different style. And being sensitive to people's different needs, the Relational Leader is likely to be able to get along with subordinates with very different ways of approaching issues. It is probably no accident that the business side of Mrs. Fields Cookies is largely run by Debbi's husband, Randy, a successful businessman in other ventures before his fifty-thousand-dollar loan launched Debbi on hers ten years ago. But his role is one of management, not of leadership, and that is a distinction that we will postpone until the next chapter.

Conceptual leaders are different in almost every way. They are sometimes so insensitive to others' feelings that they unwittingly offend them. As intuitives with an eye for the future, they are relatively uninterested in the details of operations. When they look at a particular work situation, they see the general forces that characterize it. They look at a situation and see the germ of a new situation within it. They imagine ways of doing things that have never before been tried. They live in a world of fluid outlines that can be transformed by the power of thought. Emily Dickinson wrote a poem whose first two lines could serve as a Conceptual's motto: "I dwell in Possibility,/A fairer house than Prose."

An industry analyst has recently described the airlines entrepreneur Frank Lorenzo in words that would describe many Conceptuals: "He's able . . . to look at someone else's 'home,' which is in a state of disrepair, and visualize a new coat of paint, a new roof, a few walls knocked down and a new fireplace to make it a valuable piece of property."* The "home" the analyst had in mind was an airline like TWA, but in a deeper sense it was the whole deregulated airlines marketplace, which looked like a mess to everyone else. A Lorenzo aide, who was asked what made their management team different, replied that ". . . we saw [deregulation] as an opportunity rather than as a risk."

This emphasis on possibility is extremely valuable in the early days of an organization or when the organization's environment changes radically, especially when the organization's potentialities are based on a technology. Jobs and Wozniak carried Apple from start-up to Fortune 500 list in five years with a Conceptual style of leadership. Other Conceptual leaders who were (initially, at least) only a little less successful were Adam Osborne, Sirjang Lai "Jugi" Tandon, and Nolan Bushnell.

But after meteoric starts, Osborne Computers went bankrupt; Tandon Corp. declined and is just starting to recover under new Structural leadership from IBM; and Nolan's Pizza Time Theaters, which he started after selling Atari to Warner Communications, went into Chapter 11. Conceptual Leaders have a very hard time negotiating the transition point that comes after their greatest success, which is The Venture. The transition to Making It has tripped up many a Conceptual leader.*

Magazines like *Inc.* and *Venture* regularly run articles that recount the histories of Conceptual leaders, warning that good entrepreneurs don't make good managers. The two things that such stories fail to say are (1) some entrepreneurs don't last, while others do; it is a matter of style and not of the fact that they launched the company in the first place that determines their effectiveness; and (2) the real issue isn't that entrepreneurship and management don't mix, but that leaders have as much trouble with transition as organizations do—and that many of them, in spite of talk about the future, are as unwilling to let go of the past as any of their followers are.

I don't want to leave the impression that Conceptual Leaders are only effective in the early stages of the organizational life cycle. With support from effective Structural and Relational subordinates, they can run very large and dynamic organizations. Even when the results are good, however, there is likely to be an underlying strain between their possibility-oriented style and the practical necessities of everyday operations. That Control Data's CEO William Norris has all the strengths and weaknesses of a Conceptual leader is clear from the way he has been described by one of his vice-presidents: "Hearing him tell customers about 'our new product line' (most of which is about halfway through R&D at the moment) is like standing backstage and hearing someone telling the audience that we have beautiful silk rugs for sale . . . while behind the curtain, we are still trying to get two silkworms to mate!"

At every turning point in the organization's life cycle, the leader's task is to redefine the organization's *business.* Defining that business is giving a clear form to something that is actually a confusing mixture of several different things:

1. The organization's official and public purpose: The business of Hewlett-Packard is to develop and manufacture sophisticated electronic equipment; the business of Blue Cross is to provide health insurance, and so on.

2. The organization's strategy for survival or improvement: American auto makers are in the businesses of cost containment and quality enhancement at the moment, while many biotechnological companies are in the business of getting their products approved for field tests.

3. The organization's developmental task at that phase of its life cycle: Both MCI and AT&T are in the business of Making It, but MCI is entering that business from the Venture side, while AT&T is trying to circle back into it from the Institution side.

The leader must draw upon these three dimensions of the organization—its nature, its situation, and its stage of growth—and define "what we are and what we do." The leader must do this in a way that identifies the real opportunities and dangers and is comprehensible and compelling to the rest of the organization. And it is particularly at times when one or more of these three dimensions of the organization changes and when a significant redefinition of the organization's business is consequently required that a leader is really tested. Which is to say that significant transition is the real test of leadership.

In the course of organizational growth, periods of opportunity and expansion, which demand the vision of Conceptuals and Catalysts, are succeeded by periods of consolidation that demand Structurals and Relationals. Those times of consolidation, in turn, drift toward rigidity and oppressive collectivism that in time demand new dreams of possibility and new styles of leadership to capitalize upon them.

Throughout this cycle, the demands upon leaders change. Yesterday's savior becomes today's scapegoat, and yesterday's prophet-without-honor is welcomed home as a deliverer. Some leaders make the transition inwardly, some are simply replaced, and some resist replacement so successfully that they drag the organization down with them.

It is a rare leader who understands his own limitations well enough to step aside gracefully when his time is past. Mitch Kapor is the founder of Lotus Development Corporation, the software company that has been as successful in its field as Apple has been in hardware. In a recent interview, Kapor was asked why he left Lotus after leading it to the head of the pack in five years. He replied:

> . . . as organizations grow larger, what one has to do to get them to work together changes. And what I found was that my skills are not very evenly distributed across that spectrum. At Lotus, I was really good at working one-to-one with people—or maybe two- or three-to-one . . . And I also tended to be really good at giving speeches to a hundred or a thousand people at a staff meeting. But in the intermediate stage, where you're attempting to run an organization that consists of a mass of people, with an internal structure in which authority is delegated, where other people are really carrying the ball and where one is sort of leading by coordinating—well, I'm just not very good at that.*

One could argue whether Kapor was more of a Catalyst or a Conceptual, but it is clear that he was not the Structural that he recognized Lotus needed at that point in its growth.

The most effective leaders are often those who worked their way up within a framework dictated by one phase of organizational life and led by a leader appropriate to that phase, but whose own natural style really corresponds to the demands of the new phase of organizational life. They can understand the past and honor it, but they have also let go of it, have made a new inner beginning, and can lead others through the same process.

One can watch the sequence of leadership types, each appropriate to its time, at a single organization like General Motors. William C. Durant was a Catalyst with the dream of a new kind of marketing that was segmented by the characteristics of particular groups of customers. GM's increasingly complex system, however, grew less and less appropriate to his intuitive style. A Structural leader was called for—and found in Alfred P. Sloan, Jr., who reorganized and rationalized GM's operations. In recent years, however, the Sloan legacy, liberating in its time, had become constricting and a new and more Conceptual style of leadership was required to find entirely new ways to do things. Roger Smith has tried hard to be such a leader, creating joint ventures with overseas competitors, acquiring a data-processing and an aerospace company, and creating a corporation within a corporation to manufacture the new Saturn line of cars. But GM has not moved very far or very fast, and there have been challenges by the more Catalyst style of Ross Perot's leadership—challenges that, at this writing in early 1987, have been deflected by the existing leadership.

Different times and different leadership styles. Actually, most leaders have some combination of leadership styles within them, so it is not just a case of finding the Man (or Woman) of the Hour. The situation makes the leader to some extent, in that it defines what aspect of his or her inherent style will be activated and reinforced. Leadership style is like a bridge hand, long in some suits and short in others. Perhaps in the end the right person for a particular leadership situation is defined more by the short suits than the long. In one situation, a person without vision will be useless. In another, a person without a hard-headed sense of what is actually doable is a liability. Whatever his or her style, the leader's responsibility in a time of transition is to define what is ending and what is beginning, to let go of the former and to seize the latter. It is to lead the organization through transition. For without transition, leadership would not really be needed.

8: Planning and Carrying Out a Transition-Management Project

The success of a company depends on a great many things, so I am always skeptical of those who would attribute it to a single factor. But my years in managing businesses and observing the experience of others have convinced me that the following statement is true: To be successful now and in the years to come, a company must be able to handle change.

Douglas D. Danforth, Chairman and
Chief Operating Officer,
Westinghouse Electric Corporation*

The distinction between management and leadership is one of those vexed issues that seems to get more complex as efforts are made to simplify it. The difficulty is that there is such considerable overlapping middle ground between leadership-without-management and management-without-leadership that definitions of the pure entities have a slightly unreal quality to them. In actual organizational situations, particular executives are likely to be acting as leaders in some of their actions and managers in others. So in shifting from the subject of the last chapter to the subject of this one, we are talking more about different aspects of a person's responsibility than about different people or different levels of power within an organization.

The British management expert Sir Wilfred Brown defines managers as "those who are responsible for more work than they personally can perform."* Management, by that definition, is simply whatever one must do personally to get that work done by others. From CEOs to the first-line supervisors, people have to manage the efforts of some group of people who report to them and who perform tasks for which they themselves are ultimately responsible. So everyone from top to bottom needs to be concerned with not just the management of ongoing activities but the management of the transition from one employment level, one organizational strategy, one technical process, one organizational culture, one style of leadership, or one product mix to another.

Transition management can be conducted effectively in many styles, ranging from authoritarian to participative, and in this chapter I will illustrate some of the differences between various styles. The best style is the one that fits the particular organizational culture and the individual manager's natural temperament. Every style has its strengths and weaknesses, as we shall see. But behind the diversity is a basic truth: Transition can only be managed with a consistent strategy.

The strategies we will discuss have been tested in a wide range of organizational settings and have proved to make the difference between manageable and unmanageable change. They all include four categories of activity: Preparation, Monitoring, Facilitation, and Review.

Preparation

Organizational changes are typically planned with some care, but organizational transitions are not. To put the matter another and more personal way, I am usually brought in to help an organization in transition after most of the preparation has been finished and when serious transition-related problems have already begun to threaten the success of the planned changes. This is unfortunate, because preparing for a transition usually either avoids such problems or readies the organization to deal with them effectively while they are still minor.

Yet even if an organization has reached the point where full-scale preparation is no longer possible, the subject of how to get ready for transition is still worth thinking about for a couple of reasons. First, although it may be too late to prepare a complete transition-management plan, elements of such a plan can be helpful during any phase of an organizational change. Second, transition preparedness is something that should eventually be worked into the organization's regular procedures, and every transition is an opportunity to learn what might have been done—and, therefore, what to do next time—to be ready to make a transition go more smoothly.

Whatever a manager's level of responsibility, the following list of ten actions will be helpful in getting ready for transition:

1. Describe in the most fundamental terms possible the change that is going to affect the unit in question and the resulting changes that are likely to occur within the unit as a result.

Let's say that the planned change is a reorganization. But is that the goal, or is it only a path to a more fundamental goal? Perhaps the real goal is improved collaboration between elements of the organization that are now separated from one another. In other words, make sure you're asking the right question before you put all your money on the answer. Nothing is more disruptive than throwing everyone into transition, and then having to do it all over again because the first change wasn't fundamental enough. And be sure also that you try to foresee what internal changes are going to be triggered by the external ones; if the various elements of the organization become more collaborative, what secondary changes will take place within your unit?

2. Look ahead and identify those individuals and groups that are going to be plunged into transition by these changes.

The heart of transition preparedness is foreseeing the change-induced transitions within an organization. This means studying the full field of human activity in the same way that an effective pool shot has to be plotted with the full table in mind. Far from producing unintended and unfortunate side effects, the well-designed transition management plan, like the expert pool shot, always leaves one well positioned for the next move.

Transition planning must foresee not only the likely sequence of changes, but also the transitions that will be required to make the changes work. Who is going to have to let go of what, if the changes go as planned? And who is going to have to let go of what when those changes generate secondary and tertiary changes?

It is surprisingly difficult for some people to see that the goals they are striving for are not just improvements but are actually *changes* in how things are done. They forget, therefore, that these "improvements" will force someone to let go of something. In my Transition Management Seminars, we often have to spend a considerable amount of time getting managers to see that things like "greater efficiency," "higher quality standards," or "better performance appraisal" are *changes* in how things are done, and that as clearly positive as they are, they will still cost someone something and bring someone's familiar world to an end.

3. Assess the transition-readiness of the organization—as measured by its training and communication systems, its structural flexibility, its cultural dynamism, and the morale of its personnel.

After you have foreseen the transitions that probably lie ahead of you, you need to determine how ready the organization is to make them. To assess organizational readiness and pinpoint the ways it can be improved, ask yourself these questions:

A. *How serious is the need for a change?* If the need isn't great, the cost may outweigh the value.

B. *How widely is that need perceived and understood?* Time and again, I watch organizations try to solve problems that are not even recognized as problems by those whose well-being will be threatened by the solutions.

C. *What is the organization's general openness to this kind of change?* Some organizations have a tradition of incorporating technological change easily; others reorganize so often that a re-organizational routine has developed. But many organizations don't have such a heritage, and some even take pride in resisting change.

D. *Is the organization relatively free of trauma from previous changes—particularly ones that weren't handled very well?* Old wounds begin aching again when change threatens, and old misunderstandings and mistrusts reappear to undermine present confidence.

E. *Is there a specific objective that is steering this change?* Some leaders like to stay vague "to keep their options open" or "to keep from raising expectations too much." But the result of such vagueness is that people do not know when or on what basis to act. Rumors flourish and mistrust grows in such a situation.

F. *How broad is the support for the change and how much does it polarize the work force?* Who favors it and who opposes it, and what will happen if those two factions become more antagonistic? What interests are being served in supporting and opposing the change? These questions need to be asked about stockholders, regulatory agencies, customers, suppliers, unions and professional associations, consumer and environmental groups—in short, about the whole range of potentially interested parties and not just the management and the employees.

G. *Are the current behaviors and attitudes of the leadership consonant with the change being envisioned?* As Ralph Waldo Emerson said, "What you are speaks so loudly that [people] cannot hear what you say." What about the actions of the board and the top executives? Nothing undermines a transition so much as the failure of management to follow its own rules. One of the uncomfortable functions of a Transition Monitoring Team may be to report how that failure is perceived. But it is far better to avoid the problem altogether than to have to solve it.

H. *Have there been notably successful changes in the organization's recent history?* These are worth studying—first, to determine what strategies were useful and who demonstrated natural transition-management skills, and second, to be able to build confidence by referring people back to a recent success.

I. *How effective is the communication system within the organization?* Are messages generally received? Are they believed? Is upward communication being attended to? Is there a managerial "hard pan" that makes it difficult for reliable information to "trickle down" through the organization? Transition puts communications under a great deal of stress.

J. *Is there a strong tradition within the organization of both technical and social training programs?* People are going to have to learn to behave differently, and they are going to have to develop different attitudes. Training programs are no panacea, but without them a transition-management plan is almost sure to be doomed.

K. *Does the organization have a tradition of using ritual and ceremony to mark important turning points?* Grafting new ritual onto home-grown roots works best, so it is useful to view the organization's culture as an anthropologist might, looking for existing ceremonies and symbols. These can set the tone for the new ones.

L. *Does this organization believe in taking care of its people?* If it does not, transition management may appear to be an unnecessary extra and you may have to tackle the much larger transition to a more people-oriented culture before you can approach an organizational transition with real confidence.

This is not a test, so there is no passing grade. But more than a couple of negative answers suggests that trouble lies ahead. And any negative answer indicates an area that calls for your attention.

4. Analyze the political implications of the change you are preparing to make.

In assessing the readiness of an organization for transition, you cannot avoid the issue of factionalism. Some factions are quite ready for the transition and some are not. There are essentially three approaches that one can take to this such factionalism.

The first way to counter factionalism is to redefine the situation so that erstwhile antagonists become collaborators in a redefined venture that pits them against some new antagonist rather than against one another. (This is happening in many manufacturing companies today where the management and the unionized work force transcend their old antagonisms to deal effectively with overseas competition.)

The second approach to dealing with factionalism is to submerge it in a more exciting spirit of unity that makes the factionalism seem trivial and self-defeating. This approach "aligns" former antagonists in a common direction on more fundamental level where the old oppositions no longer exist. Chrysler did this when its own survival was at stake, and People Express was successful for a time in aligning employees toward a new vision of a nonhierarchical workforce. As potential and former internal antagonists accept and work to actualize such a vision, they redefine their task as some component of the larger collaborative endeavor.

The third approach to dealing with factionalism is to take it apart piece by piece, using everything from persuasion to coercion to turn the opposition into support.* Corporate politics is little different from civic politics, and in each there is a fine line between effective political organizing and manipulation or force. Is a changed incentive system a "manipulation"? Is the threat to terminate a recalcitrant employee "coercion"? There are legal answers to these questions but from an ethical viewpoint, the main question is one of context: Are the political actions of the organization in the service of a strategic design that is going to enhance the organization and its various stakeholders, or are they in the service of someone's personal ambition?

In most organizational situations the best solutions to factionalism will draw upon all three of these strategies. Organizations ordinarily handicap themselves by focusing on one of these strategies to the exclusion of the other two. Taken by itself, the tactic of repolarizing the organizational stakeholders can degenerate into scapegoating, and it is sure to collapse if the new antagonist disappears or turns friendly. Taken alone, the alignment approach can evaporate into high-sounding phrases that everyone mouths and no one puts into practice; and in the long run (as the People Express example suggests), the "higher purpose" may dissipate into renewed squabbles once the novelty of it wears off. And by itself, the piecemeal approach can turn into a series of power plays for personal gain. Because they complement and serve as checks and balances on one another, the three approaches need to be combined.

5. Set a challenging but realistic pace for the transitions that the changes are going to require—even if the timetable for the changes themselves (as announced by the organization's leaders) is unrealistic.

It is not realistic to expect people to unplug themselves from one world, go through the no-man's-land between two worlds, and settle into their new world in a few weeks. While output cannot cease during the transition, it is completely unrealistic to expect effectiveness not to suffer for a matter of months—or, in the case of very traumatic changes, years.

6. Create a representative group of employees to serve as a Transition Monitoring Team which is charged with the job of keeping track of what is happening to people during the transition period.

This usually means creating one or more teams of people who represent the widest possible range of functions and levels within your part of the organization. (The organization as a whole should have such a team too.) No one can foresee all the effects of an organizational transition in advance, so there has to be some representative group of sensitive and well-informed people to watch the transition process as it unfolds and to identify problems and opportunities as they arise.

The Transition Monitoring Team can also serve as a focus group on which you can test the probable effectiveness of actions and communications before you make them public. I can recall a manufacturing company whose carefully researched change in work schedules was modified at the last moment, when the Transition Monitoring Team warned that the plan would be seen as an attack on a union that the company was currently trying to pacify. (See the Monitoring section of this chapter for more on Transition Monitoring Teams.)

7. Identify the new skills and knowledge that will be required by the new beginning, and find or develop training and educational programs that will provide them.

We have already discussed in chapter 5 the three kinds of training that people need to make a new beginning: training in new skills and knowledge, training in seeing their function in a new context, and training in techniques of handling self-doubt. But there needs to be a more general educational program on the subject of transition itself and how to deal successfully with it. Typically that program works on several different levels:

A. Seminars and individual coaching for top management in Leading an Organization through Transition—how to make decisions that avoid some of the serious effects of transition and how to use organizational resources to mitigate the effects that cannot be avoided.

B. Workshops and individual coaching for middle managers and supervisors in Managing People in Transition. Transitions go much better when people's direct superiors understand the effects of transition on people and have some strategies for helping people through endings, neutral zones, and new beginnings.

C. Workshops for individuals whose situations are most at risk because of the changes. I call these Making Change Work for You, and their focus is on reorienting one's worklife to capitalize on change-generated opportunities, rather than on finding a new job or even a new career that is beyond the reach of change.

8. Review the communication resources within your unit and between the unit and the rest of the organization, and make such changes in the communication channels as are necessary to keep people feeling informed and listened to.

In chapters 3 to 5, where we discussed Endings, the Neutral Zone, and New Beginnings, we covered the part played by communications during each of those three phases of an organizational transition. The only thing to add here is that managers who are preparing for an organizational transition cannot wait until they get into the transition before they think about communications. They need to evaluate the actual state of communications within their units and compare it with the level of communication that they will need to get through transition without undue disruption or delay.

Such a comparison almost always calls for some action, because few organizations have communication channels that are adequate to the demands of a transition. When GTE Sprint was preparing to relocate its headquarters after its merger with US Telecom, it launched a new company newsletter called *In Transition,* the first issue of which promised "tips on how to cope with stress and anxiety; [information on] the regions where the new company will be located; and . . . a question-and-answer [discussion] in more detail [of] what's involved in putting the two companies together."

McDonnell Douglas Astronautics, which was reorganizing a 6,500-person facility in Southern California, produced a series of videotapes to help the employees deal with the changes. In several of them the general manager explained the reasons for the reorganization; in one a management panel answered questions from a group of employees about details of the transition; and a final tape described the psychological impacts of transition and suggested techniques employees could use to minimize them. McDonnell Douglas also instituted a series of round-table lunches in which a cross section of workers met with the general manager, arranged interviews between a consultant and different groups within the facility, set up a Transition Monitoring Team, and created an ombudsman—all ways of enhancing communication from the bottom up.

9. Create incentives, both long-term and **ad hoc.** *to reward people for doing and being what the new situation requires that they do and be.*

As with communications, a comparison of existing incentives and desirable ones almost always calls for action. But before managers start setting up bonuses or other ways of rewarding people, they need to be very clear on the specific behaviors and attitudes that they want to reward. This specificity is particularly important when the transition involves important but general culture shifts, for it is easy to imagine that "being more entrepreneurial" or "managing in the Japanese way" represents something identifiable enough to be rewarded—and it doesn't.

10. Plan from the very beginning to celebrate the different phases of the transition and to represent it in symbolic ways.

Look for every possible occasion for making a symbolic statement about how things are changing and where people are in the transition. Plan little rituals to mark endings and new beginnings; plan little rituals to honor those who make the transition work; and plan little rituals that capture the essence of the new organizational world that is coming into being.

Monitoring

No matter how carefully you prepare for a transition, your preparations are handicapped by the fact that there is no way to foresee some of the effects of change or some of people's reactions to change. That is why the Transition Monitoring Team (TMT) is so valuable. Setting it up, as we noted under number 6 above, should be part of any manager's preparation for transition. But there are several ways the team can be set up that may fit a particular organization's culture more or less well and that will have somewhat different advantages and disadvantages.

Case One. In a food-packing plant, where technological changes were going to cause layoffs and a complete reorganization of the remaining workers into highly trained teams, a TMT was set up long before any of the changes was implemented. At my suggestion, the people chosen for the team represented the widest possible range of constituencies. Each of the three shifts was represented; production, maintenance, and clerical groups were represented; Latino and Anglo workers were represented; the hourly workers were supplemented by one supervisor and one manager, and the latter gave the group access to the management team and the general manager himself. The total membership, with some members representing more than one category, was twelve.

The group met twice a month during the first months in which people were assimilating the information about the changes, and later the meetings decreased to once a month. From the beginning, the TMT gave the management team a clearer sense than it had ever had of employees' reactions to the proposals about how the changes at the plant would be implemented. It warned management that its announcement had not yet sold successfully the idea that the new jobs required English—and that the requirement was perceived as an attack on the Latino workers. It alerted management to a growing bitterness against first-line supervisors who were holding back important information, both from above and below. It served as a constant critique of management's attempt to explain changes in its own plans—a critique that forced management to confront more directly its own confusions and the ambiguities it was trying to deal with. It served as a sounding board for dozens of planned announcements, so that management could tell in advance whether their intent would get across or not.

In this particular setting, an effective TMT was created by managerial selections. The manufacturing plant had a long history of showing a real, if rather paternalistic, concern for its people, and the individual workers were long-term employees who were well known to the top management. The selections were excellent, both in terms of the individual's contributions and in terms of representativeness. Because they were chosen by superiors, however, there was an initial perception by the rest of the plant that the TMT members were favored employees who were being groomed for one of the new work-team jobs. This impression disappeared gradually with time, but it was one of the prices that the company paid for what was otherwise a good way to select a valuable group of men and women.

Case Two. A medium-sized hospital, in a city where health services were dominated by several big medical centers, had begun a year earlier to launch specialized new outpatient programs to compensate for the falling rate of general inpatient admissions. Because the hospital had been in serious financial difficulties, the new programs had been launched quickly and without much internal communication or a careful assessment of their impact on existing services and personnel. By the time that the hospital's leadership began to pay attention to the situation, the staff morale had deteriorated considerably.

In this case, the TMT grew out of a transition-management seminar that I conducted. With the blessing of the hospital administrator, who was at the seminar, a group of nurses, technicians, and clerical people joined together to "check the pulse" (in the words of the hospital newsletter) of the staff. The self-selected team of fourteen members met every two weeks to assess the effects of the transition, the state of communications, and the emerging needs for training or consulting in different parts of the hospital. The team made a videotape of the transition management seminar, edited it down to an hour-long educational piece, and began showing it in the different departments of the hospital. It also encouraged the use of little rituals in the closing of several of the hospital's facilities.

This TMT was set up and went to work in a different way from the TMT in Case One, but each team fitted its situation. The hospital had not been nearly so concerned in the beginning with the disruptions and distress caused by its changes, and so it was much further along in implementing them before action was taken. A self-selected TMT proved to be a good way to tackle issues that were being forgotten in the rush toward technical and financial solutions. The hospital staff was articulate and ready to act in its own behalf, and they were more comfortable than the production workers in Case One had been to form a committee and start collecting and disseminating information. Because they were self-selected, they bore no taint of being company favorites. But by the same token, because they were not chosen, they lacked management's seal of approval. They had to work harder to establish their legitimacy in the world of department heads and program directors.

Case Three. A large and highly structured defense facility was reorganized into semi-autonomous business units, and at the same time a new set of cultural principles was announced by the chief executive of the facility's parent organization. These two efforts, though unrelated in origin or rationale, were presented as simply two sides of single change. Each effort generated considerable resistance. The first dismayed the engineers who were reassigned away from their old engineering department to one of the new business groups; the second, which endorsed participative management, disturbed everyone who believed in the old way, which was essentially a military type of organization and style of management.

From the beginning, I urged the leaders at the facility to create TMTs—the size of the organization would probably have required at least half a dozen of them—but the recommendation kept getting shelved. Meanwhile, the kinds of communications difficulties that a TMT is designed to deal with kept multiplying. Factions within the organization that felt unheard kept asking for meetings with the general manager. Some unit leaders began to report that they were afraid that good people were going to leave. The illness and accident rate rose alarmingly. The hourly production workers began to complain more than they ever had about their supervisors. Some units professed to be entirely in the dark about what was happening, and the reason for that turned out to be that some vice-presidents and directors who were unsympathetic to the changes were simply not passing on information about them. The training department, which was more concerned with turf than with training, dragged its feet in coming up with the kinds of training that would have helped the changes along.

Almost a year after the changes began and my first recommendations had been made, a TMT was set up. But rather than being a true cross section of the organization, it was chosen by the vice-presidents and made up entirely of upper-level managers. They were a sensitive and thoughtful group who became genuinely concerned about and sensitive to transition issues. But they were also busy people who were on other committees, and they met irregularly because many of them traveled extensively for the company. And in the end, they generated a sizable list of transition-related problems but were ineffective as a conduit for or evaluator of information.

The fault was not theirs. It was, in fact, no one's. This third TMT as accurately represented its organization as the other two had—which is to say that it mirrored all its difficulties: rigid hierarchy with a deep chasm between hourly and salaried workers, a command mentality that had little concern for the reactions of people to what they were told to do, and the technologist's impatience with the shortcomings of human beings. The TMT was not able to operate outside the constraints of the value system that almost everyone at the facility shared, and so it was not very successful. To have made it successful would have required a challenge to its value system that (in spite of all the talk about a culture change) most of the managers were not ready to make.

I bore some responsibility for that failure myself. It was one of my early large-scale consulting assignments, and I got swept up in the top executives' assurances that they wanted to find out what was going on and how everyone felt about the changes. They had an open-door policy there, and the general manager himself was both committed to the changes and very approachable. He listened to the complaints and was willing to act. But his willingness to respond to them lulled me into overlooking that transition-related problems were being dealt with symptomatically and not at their source.

Would an effective TMT have changed that? I don't know. But it would have connected the individual complaints with larger issues and would have built a case for the kinds of actions that were never taken—personnel changes, budget changes, new training programs, policy changes. It would have painted a more convincing picture than any outside consultant could have done of the difficulties that unmanaged transition were getting the organization into. TMTs do that, among other things, and not all leaders are ready to look at that picture.

Facilitation

Chapters 3, 4, and 5 describe what managers and supervisors can do to help people through each of the three phases of transition. But there are also more general things that you can do to manage transition successfully. They begin with making sure that you understand what a particular transition means subjectively to the people going through it before you try to "manage" anything. To "do unto others as you would be done unto" is not a Golden Rule of Management when what the others believe and need is very different from what you believe and need.

What *is* this change going to mean to those affected by it? Individually or collectively, there may be some personal history that gives this present situation a meaning to them that you will miss entirely unless you go out of your way to look for it. What seems to you like a great opportunity may look to them like a hopeless task. What you think of as a minor and one-time inconvenience may look to them like the latest example of a serious ongoing difficulty.

Managers, especially if they have been technically trained, tend to view human situations impersonally and objectively. They believe that reality just *is,* and that anyone who sees things differently is mistaken or overreacting. The idea that there are many equally legitimate subjective "realities" is hard for them to acknowledge. It is, therefore, useful for them to develop the habit of pausing before they reply to a remark that they don't agree with, and say to themselves, "That is how it feels to them and how they make sense out of what is happening." Managers need to give up on the arguments about minor facts and listen between the lines for the real message. If the person is saying something about them that they can't accept, it is helpful simply to repeat what the person is saying ("You think that I . . ."), both to show that they hear and also to get a sense of what things must look like when they are viewed from that angle.

And managers need to remember to ask questions about what people feel and why they feel that way. Only with the help of such questions and attempts to hear what is felt but unsaid can you know what losses subordinates face, what anxieties they suffer in the neutral zone, and what self-doubts block them from the new beginnings that they might make.

It is easy to imagine that when people understand one another, conflict will disappear. It doesn't, so managers should expect conflict and help people work it through, rather than trying to remove it. Conflict is not just an obstacle on what would otherwise be an open path to a satisfactory solution. Actually conflict is a natural by-product of transition.* People always have somewhat mixed feelings toward the situations around them and toward the people they take to be responsible for those situations. Most of the time they live with that ambivalence more or less satisfactorily, keeping it "in solution" like a chemical in a liquid. But change precipitates the ambivalence out of solution as strong feelings for or against something. People identify with one of those feelings and project the other, disowned feeling onto "them"—some other party to the situation, with whom they then begin fighting.

Although it is inconvenient, such conflict spotlights issues and interests, provides them with spokespersons, and in that way sorts out and prioritizes them. This helps to defuse the buried emotional charges attached to the issues. The mistaken idea that a well-managed organization is without significant conflict is similar to the idea that there is no real conflict in a good marriage. In fact, most conflict-free marriages are either still in the honeymoon phase or have suppressed their conflict, which only becomes more dangerous for being hidden. This is not to say that conflict ought to be allowed to get out of hand and to hurt people, but that it simply needs to be managed like any other natural part of the situation.

In dealing with conflicts, keep the spotlight on the interests of those involved, rather than on the positions they take. Positions are the familiar stuff of conflict: I say he's got to replace an item with the new model, and he says he won't. They say they won't take a cent less than fifty thousand, and you say you won't go over forty. Whether it's your son and the unmowed lawn, the union and the problem of temporary workers, or Russia and the question of monitoring nuclear tests, we all take *positions* like armies on a battlefield. And then, not very surprisingly, we fight. But if, instead, we could establish what everyone's *interests* are, there is a good chance that there would be a way to get those interests met.

Your son says he won't mow the lawn, but it turns out that his interests are:

1. To spend some time with his girlfriend on the afternoon when you had said the mowing had to be done.

2. To get you to hear that he thinks you are using the lawn issue to test his obedience, "as though I were still a little kid."

3. To establish his right to a "relaxed and not so damned up-tight" style of living—not "manicuring the lawn all the time!"

And your interests turn out to be:

1. Getting the lawn mowed before the company comes on Satur-day, or it goes to seed . . . whichever comes first.

2. Establishing a mutually agreed upon set of expectations about your son's assistance around the home.

3. Legitimating your standards of appearance for the public ar-eas of the house. (His room, perhaps, can be his territory.)

Now you can negotiate. Every time one of you begins to take a fixed position, one or the other can say, "Let's see. What interest is being protected here?" With another interest out on the table, the negotia-tion can proceed. (Watch out for the so-called "issues" in a conflict. Either those are really positions in fancy clothing, or they are inter-ests that someone is unwilling to own.)

The need for even this less frustrating kind of negotiation will be reduced if you spend less time trying to sell your solutions to the transition-generated problems and more time selling the problems themselves. Most managers spend a little while deciding what needs to be done and then spend a lot of time trying to convince everyone to do it. The results: First, the solution is handicapped by the hur-ried design and the lack of others' ideas; second, it is weighted down with not only its own shortcomings but also the added weight of being imposed on the people who have to carry it out.

"Selling the problem," on the other hand, means that you éducate your subordinates about what the situation really is, and what will happen if there is no change. Employees who agree that a problem is real and that it will harm their interests if it is not solved are in the market for solutions. Employees who don't, aren't.

There is a caveat here: You need to be willing to accept a better solution than yours if the employees themselves come up with one. If that prospect bothers you, then "selling the problem rather than the solution" is asking for trouble. But if that prospect bothers you, you'd better look pretty hard at what interests you are trying to protect, and why.

When you sell the problem, be honest about the extent of the change that is likely to be necessary. Don't try to soften the blow so much that you'll only have to return in a few weeks or months with new changes that have to be made. People need to have realistic information about what lies ahead of them and to believe that you will give it to them. To say that the company will have a hiring freeze but won't need layoffs—only to announce layoffs a month later—is to confuse people and lose credibility with them. "They Lied to Us" is the epitaph over the grave of many otherwise thoughtful attempts to manage change.

While I have been emphasizing ways to soften the impact of change on people, I do not want to leave the impression that change should always be minimized. As with surgery, the importance of doing no more than you need to must not become an excuse for doing less than is necessary. Far-reaching changes are often absolutely necessary for the survival of the organization on which all depend for their security, and to compromise such changes in the name of "kindness" is not only unwise but unkind. Sanford Sigoloff, the Wickes Co. CEO who saved his failing corporation through difficult surgery, has put it this way: "People [may] look at you as some sort of cold-hearted amphibian who comes out of cold, dark recesses and acts without feeling. But unless you do it, you put at risk thousands of other jobs—not just in this company but at suppliers' companies too."*

Although it is no kindness to minimize the prospect of change, you may be able to help people by showing them that a change represents a way to avoid a much more painful change later. That is what many American companies have been able to do in the past several years, when they have renegotiated labor contracts at lower wages rather than close the plant or the business. A college faculty might do the same thing when it is faced with a shrinking enrollment—rather than circle the wagons and dig in to protect themselves, they may accept the prospect of lesser transitions (new roles, new ways of delivering services, new markets) to avoid greater ones (terminations and perhaps the death of their institution). Unless that tradeoff is made explicit, however, people may resist the immediate transition without understanding that they are dooming themselves to a bigger one later.

Your task as manager is to "change the change" so that it ceases to be seen as an end to what is desirable and becomes, instead, a sacrifice that is necessary to protect what is really desirable. For protecting something always requires lesser relinquishments. It is like riding a bicycle—to go straight, you have to make constant small shifts from side to side to maintain balance.

It is essential, however, to be sure that the argument you construct really coincides with the interests of the people under you (as they experience them) rather than simply with your perception of what is good for them. "I'm doing this for your own good" and "You'll thank me for this some day" are no more effective with employees than they were when your parents used them on you. All the same, a transition really is an opportunity to unlearn outmoded behaviors and attitudes that will be a handicap in the future. Recognizing that turns change from a threat to a productive challenge.

Even if a threat can become a challenge, however, people are going to need to understand clearly the difference between what was expected in the past and what will be expected in the future. The manager should spend time studying how things were done in the old situation and what assumptions and priorities went into doing them that way. The manager can shorten the time people need to extinguish these old ways of acting and thinking by focusing people's attention on specifics rather than lumping everything together as "the old way" and telling people to put it behind them.

In a transition-management program I set up at a manufacturing facility, for example, the mechanics were going to have to make the transition from being independent repairmen who were called in when something broke to being the mechanical specialists on production teams who helped the other team members keep their machines working properly. Rather than simply showing them how to do their new jobs, the training program began by showing them the specific assumptions their old roles were based on and why those assumptions no longer fitted the needs of the production floor. The old assumptions had been

1. That all repair should be done by a mechanic, and production workers should call one when anything went wrong.

2. That the mechanic's status would be enhanced if he did not share his expertise with anyone else, because then no one else would be able to do his work.

3. That the mechanic's value would be measured by the problems he solved rather than those he helped others to prevent.

4. That the mechanic worked best as a free-floating independent, not as a team player assigned to some production unit.

In the new team-based system of production, everyone was rewarded for team performance, and Lone Ranger behavior was simply self-defeating. Personal status was enhanced by providing others with the same information that it used to be status-building to withhold. The transition faced by the mechanics was distasteful to some of them, but it was based on a need that they understood and accepted. And they made it fairly quickly.

Often the old attitudes are hard to pin down, for they are so taken for granted that no one notices them anymore. One way to smoke them out is to think of three important decisions made or actions taken in the previous few years by that particular part of the organization. (Choose at least one that went "well" and at least one that went "badly.") Then ask yourself—or, better yet, ask a group of your subordinates to help you figure out—what attitudes and assumptions shaped these decisions or actions. You may come out with items like, "Cover your tracks," "Don't take chances," "Don't be the bearer of bad news," and "Cut cost . . . at all costs." These are the things that must be unlearned, the outmoded attitudes that people have to let go of.

In trying to help people learn what they will need to know to function successfully in the new situation, managers often undermine the very changes they are trying to bring about. In the first place, they often forget that there is more to a new role than a cluster of technical skills. There is, as a VP in a large industrial facility complained to me recently, "all that esoteric crap" of social attitude and interpersonal behavior. The engineer who is reassigned to marketing and the sales whiz who is promoted to head the regional office have to learn more than technical skills. They will probably have to learn a whole new way of looking at their work, a whole new way of interacting with others, and a whole new way of making decisions.

This learning will go more easily if it is part of a well-designed plan for people to make the most out of the change. While managers need to be careful that they do not offer false hope, they need to encourage people to accept the challenge of change and spot the opportunities within it. Career development of subordinates is especially important and particularly difficult when a career ladder is being disrupted by change and the cultural norms are in flux. It requires real study of the proposed changes, their likely organizational effects, and the new career possibilities that may result from them. Managers who have done their homework can help people by showing them how the organization's transitions can be turned to their advantage. And in so doing, they can help the organization, for they will be facilitating the transitions on which its change depends and equipping employees to deal more successfully with change in the future.

Review

From the moment a manager sets a plan into motion, he or she needs to begin reviewing its results and deciding what is working and what is not. In the process, a manager will inevitably begin to think about redesigning some of the policies, procedures, roles, and symbols that are hindering the organization's ability to make and to survive transitions. Creating the transition-ready organization is a subject in itself, and I have devoted the last chapter of this book to it.

I have one more piece of advice on managing a transition successfully, and it is a very difficult one for some of the best managers I deal with to hear: Take care of *your* transition before you try to help anyone else deal with theirs. It is "Physician, heal thyself!"—not just because that is fair or honest, but because the physician's disease, if it is denied, is likely to reappear in more malignant form in the patient. Managers rationalize their denial in several ways: (1) "My position's secure. It's these guys under me who are up for grabs!" (2) "I don't have time to worry about myself. I'll get around to that when things calm down here." (3) "I'm not paid to worry about myself. My job is to take care of other people." But they all add up to the same thing—the refusal to recognize that the transitions going on in your part of the organization are going to mean transition for you too.

As we noted in chapter 3, denial is a natural first reaction to actual or threatened loss. So the fact that you may be denying that you are in transition is not surprising, nor is it necessarily a bad thing in itself. But when that denial continues for any length of time, it undermines your effectiveness as a manager. Your own anger and sadness and anxiety stay bottled up, and in that state you will find it very difficult to deal constructively with those feelings in others. You may overreact to the feelings and end up punishing people for what are only the natural and temporary signs of the grieving process. Or you may not even notice that people are acting angry or sad or anxious—until their feelings have escalated to the point where your group's effectiveness is seriously damaged.

In spite of your denial, it may in fact be you yourself who are most at risk in the organizational transition. In the old days, the workers came and went, but management rode out most of the bad weather. No longer. For one thing, companies cannot cut labor costs enough without making major reductions in the white-collar labor force. For another, the new models of organizational structure that are popular today are all management-light, with decision making being decentralized and chains of command being shortened. And finally, what many of the so-called laborsaving machines "save" is the need for supervision more than labor in the hands-on sense.

A recent *Business Week* survey of Computer Integrated Manufacturing (CIM) can stand as typical of the way robotics and other laborsaving procedures affect management: "Surprisingly, the chief goal of CIM is not to eliminate direct-labor costs," concluded the study.

> For most products, those savings would fall far short of justifying the huge investments required . . . Instead, CIM's primary benefits come from automating the flow of information through a factory. That eliminates not only direct labor [which typically runs between 5 and 15% of production cost] but also the bulk of costs—usually in the area of 45% —attributed to indirect labor, middle management, and other overhead.*

As though that weren't enough, the managers who survive these changes are going to find their responsibilities, their authority, and their status changed. Old-style authority is on the way out, and team leadership is in. Being firmly placed in the organizational hierarchy is on the way out, and being mobile and adaptable is in. Being the possessor of special information is on the way out, and being a channel for the transmission of information is in. So even if your employment is not being threatened, your traditional identity is changing rapidly. You are in transition, and your own effectiveness is going to suffer if you do not face that fact and deal with it consciously. The next chapter will give you a plan for doing this.

PART THREE

*SURVIVING
THE
CHANGE
EPIDEMIC*

9: Making Change Work for You

> It was a complete shock. My wife and I always thought I would stay with Safeway until I retired . . . I'm very bitter. I always stood up for the company and did what they wanted me to do.
>
> Robert Markell, accountant, Denver

> I used to think that careers were like a freeway system, complicated maybe, but all laid out and comprehensible. But today, they're pure cross-country—no paths, no signs, just bushwhacking and making up the route as you go along.
>
> Margaret Walls, product manager,
> food processing, Chicago*

These are hard times for employees. Every week or so I cut out another article about people who got pushed out the organizational door and can't get back in. A forty-nine-year-old man who used to earn $36,000 a year selling robotic work stations is today driving a borrowed car to his job interviews and sleeping on friends' sofas. A fifty-seven-year-old marketing executive, whose semiconductor firm failed, talks about his family's inability to believe that he couldn't get work if he really tried. His briefcase bulges with rejection letters, and he says grimly, "My marriage is one minute to midnight." In parts of the industrial heartland, there are whole towns full of such people.*

For those who aren't laid off, the long-term prospects are not much better. The middle rungs on the management ladder are being knocked out, and fewer and fewer people can look forward to the kinds of predictable promotions that once served to motivate people in the organizational world. They call it "demassing" or "downsizing" or "getting rid of the fat," but in the end it simply means that the career paths are destroyed. "So many managers have been demoted," an Exxon employee complains, "there is a layer on top of me—people in their forties and fifties—that I will never get through."*

Every time an organization receives a jolt from the outside, little avalanches of change inside the organization begin to push people around and bury them. Corporate raider Asher Edelman mounted a takeover bid for Lucky Stores, the large western grocery chain. The Lucky board decided to stave him off by buying back company stock, and to raise money to do this they shut the company's discount chain, Gemco, and sold the assets. Gemco had food departments, and the managers of those departments were offered jobs in Lucky Stores. Charles D. Lightfoot, had to lay off his Gemco staff south of San Francisco and move across the Bay to Vallejo, where he took over the Lucky supermarket there. To make room, the manager of that market was demoted to head clerk, with a 28 percent cut in pay. Since then, the demoted manager has had to take time off on disability pay and see a psychiatrist for treatment of anxiety. "I really liked my job," he said. "It's like a low blow . . . But let's face it. I need a job."

The human cost of change is staggering, and in the end the federal and state governments are going to have to remodel their unemployment benefits and their retraining programs to deal with it. The organizations themselves must also do far more than they are now doing to protect people from some of the most destructive effects of constant organizational change, and as we shall see in the next chapter there are a number of things that they can do—things that will benefit both the employees and the companies themselves.

But such remedies can move through our organizational world only very slowly, and in the meantime we need something that individuals themselves can do to deal with the chaos that they are faced with. We need personal strategies for dealing with change. It isn't enough for individual workers to get retrained after their old skills become outmoded, since their new skills may be rendered obsolete even faster than the old ones were. It is not enough to help people to find a new job, because that new job may be squeezed out in the next round of restructuring or layoffs. People need something more basic—ways to make change work for them rather than against them.

People sometimes say that there aren't good jobs available anymore, but the problem is deeper than that. It is not just that the *good* jobs are disappearing, but that *jobs* as such are disappearing. For jobs are not an element of nature. They are a social artifact, the result of an economic situation that came into existence hardly more than a century ago. Up to that time, the work lives of the majority of people had always been made up of a variety of tasks, performed for themselves or someone else or several other people, on a schedule that varied with the season, and in whatever places were appropriate to the task in question. During the nineteenth century, however, factories and offices began to absorb more and more people, until finally the typical person's work had become a full-time employment, on a regular schedule at a fixed place, performing a standardized set of operations.

You can trace this change in the meaning of the word *job*. Today, when we talk about people's *jobs*, we are talking about their social position, the source of most of their income, a large part of their social status, and much of their subjective sense of who they are. But *job* has been used that way for only about a century. Before that time it meant "a piece of work, or transaction, done for hire or with a special view to profit" or any "small definite piece of work done in the way of one's special occupation or profession." In other words, one didn't "have a job"; one "did jobs." We still use the old sense in phrases like "jobs around the house" or an "odd-job man."

The same forces that created modern *jobs* are today destroying them. Organizations are, in the wonderful jargon of the social sciences, "disaggregating," coming apart. Functions that once belonged to one kind of organization are taken over by another. Functions that were once carried out within one organization are now scattered among many. Just as the organization has grown more fluid, the fixed units of specialized, synchronized, and centralized labor that we have called *jobs* have begun to disappear. There is still plenty of *work* to be done, of course. But *jobs*, in the sense that we have been used to them for a century, are no longer the best way to get that work done and they are not, therefore, any longer the building block of a viable career or the source of long-term security.

This is not the first era in which the social positions that once spelled security have dissolved. At the end of the Crusades the political and social forces that had held the armies together began to disappear, and the armies "disaggregated" into what came to be called *free lances* (or *lancers),* unattached individuals trying to find new places to do the work that they knew how to do. Unfortunately, what they knew how to do was to fight and kill, and so their contribution to the social life of their day was extremely disruptive. Fortunately, the skills that today's free lances bring with them are more constructive. But if they cannot find ways to use them, the free lances will disrupt our society just as they did seven hundred years ago.

In an age of disaggregation like ours, people long to find a safe haven beyond the reach of the chaos in the workplace. But, except in unusual and isolated cases, security is less likely to come from escaping change than it is from finding a way to capitalize on the opportunities it creates. It is often impossible to see just where a particular change will end up taking things, so a career strategy built on prognostication is unlikely to serve one as well as one hopes it will. The people who headed for Houston when oil and Sunbelt living were sure bets, or the people who headed for Silicon Valley when everyone said that tomorrow belonged to computers and a California lifestyle discovered how misleading predictions can be.

Today's workers should pay less attention to the changes that the futurists claim to foresee and more attention to the process of change itself. The first thing that they need to understand about change is that it breaks things up, and the second is that this disintegration reduces mass and creates surface. The big, solid organizational units of yesterday provided a stable structure in which security consisted in being as near the core as possible. The old metaphor for precariousness was being "marginal," near the edge. When hard times came, they trimmed the edges off things and left the center: Last hired, first fired; back to basics; cut the frills.

But in a rapidly changing situation the edges are not where the danger is. They are where the action is. One of the most significant words of this era is *interface.* It means more than "boundary," for that word refers primarily to enclosing and excluding. *Interface* means "where the surface of one thing meets the surface of another." It is less like a dividing line and more like a permeable membrane, and the action at the interface is the interplay, the communication, the mutual influence that goes on between societies or organizations or departments or teams that are side by side. The interface is where things are filtered and slowly and selectively let in or out. The interface is where the vital relationships are established that are necessary for survival in a world of increasing interdependency.

What does that mean in practical terms? It means that in today's organizations people who position themselves along these interfaces are quite literally on its "growing edge." Those who do so are the interpreters of one side to the other: the adapters, the mediators, the brokers, and the facilitators.* So, Rule 1 in Making Change Work for You is *Head for the edge.*

The people who work along the interface between the organization and its external environment are the sources of all the information that is needed to survive in this rapidly changing world. An organization that does not pick up the early signs of shifts in consumer values, that does not recognize quickly a threat from a new competitor, that does not grasp readily the significance of governmental decisions—is simply not going to survive long. Tomorrow's successful organization is going to need a much more sensitive and elaborate "sensory system" than most organizations have today, and in the end that sensing is done by individuals who work at some interface between the organization and some other entity.

People along the interface also function in reverse as the interpreters of the organization to its environment. The people in public relations, public information, and advertising do this on an official basis, and it is no accident that these fields have grown immensely in the past several decades. But the point is not that an advertising firm or a public information department is where the action is. The point is that the interface is the place where change is creating work, and that individuals who can understand what needs to be done there will be well rewarded for their efforts.

At all the internal interfaces, one finds the same increase in significant action. Wherever one department or one constituency within the organization meets another—marketing and production, industrial products and consumer products, management and labor, middle- and upper-level management—new and pressing problems are arising. With each change that takes place on one side of the interface, the balance and the communication between the two entities changes and needs to be reestablished. People are jostled into transition. Things need to be done.

Along these interfaces the staffing is often minimal, since most organizational charts represent a response to yesterday's issues more than to today's. Anyone trying to capitalize on the opportunities offered by change will discover three very important things about the understaffed interfaces of the organization: (1) There is work there that the organization needs done and, therefore, the chance to make oneself valuable; (2) Wherever there is understaffing, people's roles tend to be loosely defined and subject to change, so one can create a place for oneself more effectively than elsewhere; and (3) Wherever people's roles are loosely defined, they are likely to be working at least partly outside the area of their specialized training, and so more tolerant of others who are moving outside their own area of expertise.

Working at the interface also requires a different approach from what is appropriate in traditional organizational positions. Since much of the work along the interface isn't yet incorporated in formal roles, it may be easily overlooked or misunderstood by anyone who is role-oriented. So the person needs to become attuned to "work needing to be done" and forget formal roles or jobs. Most of the new wave of unemployed managers in this country are people who had jobs that only a few years earlier everyone had agreed were very secure. Security in turbulent times comes from doing something important for the organization, not from filling a long-standing position. So Rule 2 in Making Change Work for You is, *Forget jobs and look for work that needs doing.*

A corollary of this work-mindedness is that people who do what needs doing and don't worry too much about whether it represents a traditional *job,* end up doing things that would be unlikely to be found in any one job description. In traditional career development, that would not be good strategy, because it wouldn't put you solidly on any of the various career paths. In Department A you'd be considered a B, in Department B you'd be seen as a C, and in C an A. You'd be the organizational Man Without a Country. But in the organization in transition, you're practicing what any kind of investor (and you are investing your time) is urged to do when things are changing in unpredictable ways—you are diversifying. Rule 3 of Making Change Work for You, therefore, is *Diversify your efforts into several different areas of activity.*

There are different levels of diversification, all the way from people who divide their time among several different projects within an organization to the person who is engaged in two or three (or six or eight) part-time ventures with several organizations. For the past four or five years I have studied people in the latter category, people with what I call "Composite Careers," and I have come to believe that they are vocational pathfinders in a sense that few people realize. Some things about their careers are worth incorporating into the careers of anyone who is seeking to diversify his or her efforts within a single organization.

Diversification works by making the worker less vulnerable to the dislocations caused by organizational change. Like diversified investors, people with composite careers can balance a loss in one area with a gain in another. Consequently, they are not subject to the total disasters faced by people who have all their bets on one square. Diversification "braids" your career line out of several strands, so that the whole will hold even if one or two of the parts break. The traditional job-based career, in contrast, is more like a string of pearls. It will fall apart if its continuity is broken.

Diversification builds in security in another way as well, for the mix of activities in a composite career is always changing and so the vocational center of gravity is constantly being relocated for stability. Last month it was 30 percent of your time here, 20 percent there, and 50 percent in the other place; but this month it is 40, 55, and 5. You're always refocusing your efforts on the places where you can do what really needs doing, and so a composite career is constantly being modified to take advantage of the opportunities presented by change.

Diversifiers are unlikely to be bored and worn down by endless and meaningless routine. They are constantly tackling new challenges and expressing themselves in several different ways that match the variety of their real interests. In a sense, they are taking the fact that most people have several different careers during their work lives, and they are pursuing those multiple careers simultaneously. They do not have to go through the trauma of completely changing careers, however, because through diversification they are changing them continually.

Because of their multiple organizational affiliations diversifiers, replace the little knot of attachments that the traditional job fosters with a far-flung network of relationships. To put it crudely, the diversifier has lots of contacts. People who work at an edge become networkers by necessity. They turn to those networks for information or resources that are not available elsewhere, and they use them to do work that could not be accomplished otherwise.

Those same networks are there for their own use when and if they need career assistance. In talking to interface workers, you are likely to hear them say that they found their new position because they got a call from "a guy I knew when I was liaison between . . ." To the extent that you get ahead because of who you know, being a diversifier gives you an advantage because it provides you with many more sources of information and support.

For all its advantages, diversification has some costs too. It forces you to adjust to several different organizational subcultures and the expectations of several different superiors. It destroys the old, comfortable assumptions about there being some single right way to do things, and it throws you back on your own understandings and intuitions much more than work in a traditional job does. Some people like that very much, but others find it anxiety-producing.

Diversification is also difficult for people who want everything to be in good order at the end of the day, because there is always too much to do and new things always arise before the old ones are disposed of. Operating at the interface is a little like being one of the plate spinners in the Chinese circus; they get a dinner plate spinning on top of a vertical dowel, then set it on a table and get the next spinning, and the next, and the next, and all the way down to the end of the table until a dozen plates are spinning atop dowels. But no sooner are they finished at one end of the table than the first plate down at the other end of the table is wobbling wildly, about to crash, and they have to dash the length of the table and whip it up again. There is a lot of dashing up and down the table when you have a diversified career.

There are certain skills that people who want to make change work for them must develop. Some of these skills are still suspect in most parts of the organizational world, because they are not the ones that have been traditionally associated with being a good employee. But many of the traditional good employees are being laid off now. And with these "good" employees is going the assumption about employment—the psychological contract between employer and employee—that has formed the basis of most careers. In the past, most workers took it for granted that if they gave their best efforts and were loyal, their employer would take care of them. But there are simply no longer places for all of these people, and the psychological contract is being broken. The bitterness that is spreading through organizations in transition today comes from a sense of betrayal—a betrayal all the more painful because organizations continue to espouse the old values as though the bond were still intact.

As often happens with rapidly changing situations, there has been a culture lag within most organizations. When organizations in transition reconsider what really makes employees effective, they are likely to realize that creating a cadre of employees who can make change work for them is worth any organization's time. Otherwise it is like having your boat crewed by nonswimmers—they are so preoccupied with their own survival that they cannot keep their minds on the task of getting the boat through the storm.

The skills necessary to turn change into a personal opportunity begin with the ability to break free of the old way of seeing things and look at them in a new way. Ralph Waldo Emerson once said that if you don't believe that the world could look different, you need only bend over and look back at something through your legs. You need to turn things upside down occasionally to stop seeing the pattern that you've imposed on them and let them take a new shape.

What you need is illustrated in the story of the Zen patriarch who was deciding which of two students he ought to designate as his successor. The three of them meditated silently for several hours. Then, without warning, the patriarch took out a fan and handed it to one of them. The student looked surprised, but realized that he was supposed to do something with the fan, so he opened it, fanned himself a few times, and handed it back to the master. The latter passed it to the second student. The latter took it, opened it, fanned himself, closed it and stuck it down the back of his collar where he used it as a backscratcher, then brought it out, opened it flat, put a cracker on it as though it were a tray and held it out to the master. The master chose the latter as his successor.

Everything can be looked at in new ways. Take some situation that is a problem for you, and consider all the different ways you could look at it.

- Take the good aspects of it and find what's bad about them. Many of our difficulties in changing situations come from not recognizing the side effects of our intentions and actions. Take your organization's strengths, for example, and look at them as though they were sources of weakness. In changing times, yesterday's advantage turns into tomorrow's handicap with alarming frequency.

- Take the bad aspects and find what's good about them. This too has considerable practical value, for we seldom allow ourselves to see how our difficulties protect us from things we don't want to deal with. Eric Berne even gave that tactic a name, calling it the game of "Wooden Leg" after someone who excuses his ineptness by saying, "What can you expect of a man with a wooden leg?"* Overworked executives, for example, might ask what the murderous schedule and the inability to find time for family or recreation is saving them from.

- Exaggerate the details of the problematical situation, making minor things critically important and reducing central issues to relative insignificance. Many emerging problems are at first evident only in little details. And the fact that we consider something "insignificant" may say more about how we define the problem than it does about the problem itself. A couple of resignations may be an insignificant detail in the big picture of a productive department, but if it is also a department in which people are feeling undervalued and overworked, then the detail may be a forewarning of a big picture that isn't going to look so good.

- Turn situations around, making the passive parts active, results into causes, and means into ends. Salespeople talk to customers differently when they see them as people who actively need something rather than simply as the passive audience for their sales pitch; executives see ways to improve work conditions when they picture their organizations as systems specifically designed to create stress in employees; and leaders who can imagine that an employee suggestion system has become an end in itself may be able to see why it is not a more successful means of producing innovation.

If these shifts in perspective are difficult for you at first, remember that you have been barraged for years with demands that you see things in the same way everyone else does. Keep working on it. If you think that it is silly to spend your time on such things, you may be in real trouble, however. You're sure to be missing real opportunities in your situation by sticking so close to what is generally agreed to be "reality" that you're failing to see opportunities for improvement.

To make change work for you, you also need to become *flexible.* To deal with the transitions that disrupt work lives, you've got to be ready to let go of the familiar, ready to let go of outlived dreams and assumptions. You have to be ready to do things in unfamiliar ways and to let yourself feel the excitement of trying new things. And you have to be ready to roam the wilderness of the neutral zone, keeping your eyes open for signs and resisting the temptation to turn around and retrace your steps back to the past. To help yourself become more flexible, these brief exercises will be useful:

- Take a few minutes and ask yourself, "What's it time to let go of in my life now?" The things it may be time to let go of are not the external details of your life, though some of them might indeed have lost their meaning and usefulness, but those less tangible inner things (dreams, self-images, values and goals, assumptions about what has to be) that make the external things make sense. A forty-year-old middle manager may realize that it is time to stop pretending that he's on the way to the top of a big corporation. A thirty-year-old assistant VP may realize that it is time to let go of the image of herself as someone who needs a paternalistic mentor. A fifty-year-old supervisor may realize that his blue-collar self-image no longer fits the reality of his high-tech role and is holding back his career.

- Sometime between now and bedtime, do something that you never do, something unfamiliar, something that "isn't like you." The easiest way to do this is to choose a situation where you have fallen into the habit of always doing the same thing—and choose consciously to do something else. Try doing that at least once every day for the next week. Start with trivial things, like the route you take to work or what you have for lunch, and then move on to bigger things, like how you handle an interpersonal situation or how you plan out your work day. You will learn about your own resistances to innovation, and you will also begin to soften those resistances.

Flexibility provides the ability to respond to the new and often poorly defined signals that one finds along any interface between two entities. But before you can respond, you need to be aware of the signals. *Sensitivity* is, therefore, the next quality that people need to develop if they want to learn to make change work for them. You need to become more sensitive to both external signals and internal ones.

The external signals cue you in to the subtle first indications of significant change in the outer world, and the internal ones alert you to the kinds of changes within you that may mean you need to revise your own goals or change the means you are using to reach them. The clues provided by your inner reactions to a changing situation may also alert you to external factors that you cannot perceive directly. Many an executive has spent months wishing that he or she had taken more seriously the queasy feeling in the pit of the stomach that was his only warning that something about a deal just wasn't right.

- Start keeping a notebook in which you jot down all those apparently insignificant but puzzling little pieces of information you pick up every day. If you wonder why one person's sales figures are well above (or below) everyone else's, write it down. If you find yourself wondering what effects Detroit's next round of incentives to car buyers will have on your customers' spending, write it down. If your interest is piqued by statistics showing that many more adult children are living with their parents today than in the recent past, write it down. If someone tells you that one part of manufacturing is having trouble meeting its quota and can't seem to find out why, write it down. Then every week, go over the daily entries—and skim back over earlier ones if you note a similarity to some related fact you recorded earlier. There are nuggets of information to be found in this apparently useless gravel, so don't be disappointed if your first efforts fail to turn up anything valuable. It may be only on the third or fourth notation of some trend-related fact that you catch on to what is beginning to happen on the other side of the interface.

- Set aside ten minutes tomorrow and spend the time doing nothing—not doing odds and ends or listening to music or chatting with a friend, but doing nothing, just being passive and attentive to what's going on inside you. Do the same thing the next day and the next. As you get used to these pockets of emptiness, you will find yourself becoming less impatient to get on with things and you will become more sensitive to the ideas and intuitions that are covered up by the busyness of everyday activity. You may find that you've been worrying about something for a week, but at such a low level of awareness that you really didn't know it until you stopped and listened. You may find that there are things you'd like to do—things you weren't even conscious of. This exercise also teaches you about how you react to unstructured time and, therefore, to the neutral zone as well.

Of course, you can bring something up into your awareness but fail to understand its significance. This happens most often because you file away the information before you have really thought about it. People who want to learn to make change work for them cannot afford to judge things prematurely.

In developing your awareness and restraining your prejudgment you are looking for some need in your organization or its customer base that is not currently being filled. In his recent *Innovation and*

Entrepreneurship, Peter Drucker has given dozens of examples of individuals and organizations that did that in the marketplace. Gifford Pinchot III has provided comparable examples of people who did the same thing within their organizations and has coined the term *intrapreneurship* to describe that kind of opportunity-mindedness. But while these examples are inspiring, they are also a little overwhelming. They suggest that the process requires some unusual degree of technical competence and a great deal of self-confidence. How many of us are going to be able to produce an oscilloscope—or even Scotch tape—no matter how well it would fill an unmet need?

Actually, the opportunity-mindedness that is required to make change work for you is not a special gift. It is simply a habit, established by decision and strengthened by practice, of looking for things that are not working as well as they could be; of looking for needs that are not being met; and of looking for promising beginnings that no one is following up. When this results in new products or services, we call it entre- or intrapreneurship, but when the same opportunity-mindedness results simply in people finding new positions for themselves within a changing organization, we do not have a good name for it. There is nothing that serves one better when an organization is being restructured than this quality, which is made up of personal initiative and a problem-mindedness, and which can be called an *enterprise.*

Like many other personal qualities, enterprise is something some people have by nature. But other people, for whom it is not nearly so natural, have developed it through practice. The secret to doing so is to develop its two elements. Initiative is something that gets easier with practice, and all but the most dyed-in-the-wool procrastinators can develop it. Very often, it takes only a small internal push to get oneself to cross the line between inaction and action, and unless that line is crossed, you won't be able to act in your own behalf. (During the coming week, keep track of those situations in which you feel an impulse to act but talk yourself out of it. Find out what is standing in the way of your initiating more things.)

But initiative itself is not enough, for without a problem-identifying and problem-solving approach, initiative can work against you. People who are full of initiative, but product- or service-minded rather than problem-minded, know just what you need. They are usually impatient with your inability to recognize the need, and may see that you get "what you need" even if they have to pin you flat on your back to do it. Their product- or service-mindedness begins with what they happen to be selling. Problem-mindedness, on the other hand, would begin with what you are trying to accomplish and what stands in the way of accomplishing it.

Look around your organization—both the immediate world of your department and the larger world of the organization as a whole—and ask yourself what needs are not getting met. Look particularly for new situations where internal or external changes have left holes or thin places in the staffing. Giving the understaffed group a hand, even if it means a little more work than you want to carry in the long run, is a way that many people begin to insert themselves into a new and as yet undefined role. If the need is really there, it is often not very difficult to convince the powers in charge that their task would be simpler and more successful if someone could provide them with a way to deal with the problematical situation.

Most of the skills used in conventional job hunting are useful to people who want to make change work for them. Networking provides you with the information about unmet needs and the route to the people who have the power to hire someone to fill them. Self-marketing is necessary to build a good case that you are the answer to that person's problem. Negotiating skills are essential in working out the details of the new assignment, and in some cases of its pay as well.

The goal is not a traditional job, however, but employment to help solve a problem. Since that "employment to help solve a problem" is likely to acquire a title pretty quickly and a place on the organizational chart, it may seem as though we are quibbling in distinguishing it from a "job." But in the mind of the seeker, the two are quite distinct. Job hunting means looking for slots in the organization that have already been designated as "jobs," while the activity we are here talking about means looking for situations that are not yet "jobs."

Because networking, self-marketing, and interviewing are strategies that are well covered by Richard Bolles's *What Color Is Your Parachute?* and its dozens of successors, it is not worth repeating their advice here. But such career guides tend to leave the impression that job hunting is an occasional necessity which, when successful, ceases to be relevant to your career—at least until the next time you are laid off. Few of them emphasize that the tactics they suggest must be worked into the very fabric of a transition-worthy person's career on an everyday basis if you are to stay employed in a rapidly changing organization.

To turn change into an ally, people need to develop a set of habits and use them in the conduct of their daily work. Tomorrow's successful career is likely to be a braid of successful projects, and one must be constantly preparing the soil in which the next project will take root. Such planning requires that certain things be kept up to date:

- A file of "accomplishments" and descriptions by others of the part that you played in them. If you are going to convince me that you can solve my problem, you'd better be ready to demonstrate to me that you have solved other problems in the organization before and that some people whose names or positions I would recognize have said that you saved the day for them. Such a list also helps to build up your self-confidence, and that is important because free lances do not get the same kinds of sustained feedback and reinforcement from their work that people in traditional jobs do.

- Contact lists: names and numbers of people within the organization with whom you've worked. Such a list requires you to keep track of people as they move around within and outside the organization. But the keeping track has a payoff of its own, which is that you know much more about the needs of the organization and others in its field than you would if you lost contact with these people.

- A personal public relations effort. Some interface jobs are very visible, but many are not, since they do not form a link in the ordinary reporting chains. There are many ways to compensate for this. Andrew Sherwood, an executive recruiter, suggests looking for opportunities to make speeches at industry association meetings or volunteering to help the organization's United Fund drive. You can also wangle an appointment to a task force. And you can send information about the meeting, the drive, or the task force (with a discreet mention of your role) to the organization's newsletter. You do need, however, to keep the focus on the group rather than on you so that you don't appear too self-serving.

There is another side to the business of capitalizing on the opportunities provided by an organization in transition, and that is that you must know yourself well. An unmet need is not really an "opportunity" if you lack the abilities or the motivation to fill it, or if it leads you afield from the path toward the goals that are important to you. Many an otherwise exciting career has been damaged by poor decisions that came from failures of self-understanding.

Understanding yourself is a huge undertaking that is never complete. Yet you do not have to wait forever to gain some of its benefits, for you can avoid many pitfalls by assessing yourself in the following ways:

Style. As we said in the chapter on leadership, people really do have different styles, and the four basic styles we discussed there can be useful to you. Are you by nature a future-oriented Conceptual or Catalyst, someone who is always dreaming of new possibilities but is a little vague about the present particulars? Even if there is a terrific unmet need for a bookkeeper over in Purchasing, you probably aren't cut out to fill it. And if you are a present-oriented Structural or Relational, the opportunity to set up a Strategic Planning Office may not be one you ought to seize unless it is the tangible "office" rather than the more abstract "planning" part of the task that you are going to focus on.

The research that has been done on style and careers is very interesting, for it shows that certain types do cluster in certain fields. Yet there is no simple one-to-one relation. A Relational is likelier to become a pediatrician than a Conceptual is, but if the latter is really motivated, he or she may do wonderful work as a researcher on childhood diseases or as the medical administrator of a pediatric clinic. Your style, in other words, tells you more about what aspects of a task you will be best at than it does about whether or not a specific field is right for you. (For more on style, including a test to ascertain your own, see David Keirsey's *Please Understand*

Me. Isabella Briggs Myers's *Gifts Differing* provides very interesting correlations between type and career choice.)*

Abilities. When people consider leaving the familiar world of jobs for the strange world along an interface and the multiple roles of a composite career, they are likely to be hampered by "the experience trap." You have probably been struggling with this trap since you were trying to get your first job and found that it always seemed to require prior experience in that field. So now you are thinking of leaving the Accounting Department or Sales and you ask yourself what you know how to do: Accounting and Sales, of course. The dilemma gets especially painful if your old position simply disappears, as it does when they close a whole department. You are a crackerjack production supervisor—and then they send all the production over to Taiwan!

I faced this situation when I left teaching, for I honestly believed that teaching was all that I knew how to do. It wasn't until I stopped thinking of "teaching" and started thinking of what I was actually doing every day at the college that I began to identify my *abilities.* I was good at helping people to understand what they were trying to do; I was an effective planner of new ventures; I was a good adviser to people who were trying to organize new projects; I could write and speak well; and I loved to explain things. These abilities could be used in a thousand roles, I realized. As long as I could demonstrate that I had them and show how they would solve someone's problem, I could always find a place for myself.

To identify your own abilities, ask yourself a couple of questions:

- What do you actually do in your work? Break the role down into its components: analyzing data, dealing with difficult people, persuading others to join a project, keeping track of inventories, fixing things that no one else can fix, making tough decisions, helping people find the resources they need. There should be at least a half-dozen of them, and they are the abilities you are currently using at work.

- What abilities do you use in your nonwork life—in keeping the household going, in a volunteer job, at your church or club, in a hobby? Add these to your list. Watch out that you don't trap yourself in too narrow definitions, e.g., "I can do my taxes" or "run a Scout meeting" or "make a soufflé." In each case, the abilities are what it takes to do those things, not the things themselves. You will probably repeat some of the items from your previous list, but you should also turn up three or four additional ones.

- Finally, think back at least ten years and choose a couple of work or nonwork accomplishments from your past that you were proud of. They need not be big things or things you would be proud of doing today, just things that you did well and that made you feel good when you did them. It's a good idea if one of them comes from your youth, before you got locked into work roles. Perhaps you sold more magazine subscriptions than anyone else in your home room, perhaps you climbed Mount McKinley, perhaps you conquered a stutter or were photo editor on your high school yearbook. Once again, break the accomplishment down into its component abilities and add any new ones to your list.

The abilities you identify can be combined into many different clusters, and so can serve you in many different kinds of settings. Some of them can be strengthened by further training or experience, and all of them must be backed by actual examples if they are to be convincing to anyone else. When the time comes to market yourself to someone who has an unmet need, you will know what to say when they ask you what you can do for them.

The next aspect of self-knowledge that you will need to understand is your own *motivation*. What interests you most, makes you feel productive, brings out your energies and talents, turns you on? This is not quite the same as asking what you like to do—it's more like asking what stimulates you to put effort into something.

Is it financial reward or personal recognition?

Is it status that everyone can recognize or power that only insiders can see?

Is it the chance to be creative or to be responsible for something?

Is it to feel challenged or secure?

Is it to work closely with others or to be on your own?

Is it to be part of a big or a little team?

Is it to use your body or your mind?

Is it to solve social problems or technical ones?

Is it to figure out the solution or to make it actually work?

You will find these questions easier to answer if you think first of a half-dozen times in your life when you really loved what you were doing. These "high moments" don't need to have anything to do with your job or your career. When you have selected them, go through them one by one to see what they tell you about the conditions and goals that motivate you.

Resources: So far we haven't mentioned degrees or ten years of experience in advertising or research labs. This is because very few people actually do badly at their work because they lack these credentials, which sound important, and, on job-applications, are. But the organizational world is full of people who didn't get where they are because of them, and if you are looking for work that needs doing and not just a job, then they are not as essential as most people think they are.

Yet they are not things to overlook either, for they represent resources that you can capitalize upon. If you do have a doctorate in electrical engineering, you have a shot at certain appointments that you wouldn't have without one. But you could say the same thing about speaking Chinese because that was your family's second language. Or being a former bodybuilding champion, or knowing hundreds of jokes, or having $75,000 equity in your house.

All of these resources may or may not be useful to you, depending on the situation. If you wanted to start a new Nautilus franchise, the equity in your house and a bodybuilding championship would be more important resources than a Ph.D. If your company is getting interested in developing trade ties with the Orient, your speaking knowledge of Chinese wins hands down. There is hardly any educational, financial, personal, or physical fact about you that could not, under the right circumstances, be a resource. All you can do is list as many of your resources as you can, and then remember them when particular unmet needs begin to arise.

It is the creative combinations of your *style,* your *abilities,* your *motivators,* and your *resources* that qualify you as the answer to someone's needs as they emerge during organizational change. As long as your identity is tied to an existing job, you are unlikely to be able to imagine yourself doing anything significantly different or to convince someone else that you could. But if you redefine your identity in terms of these four attributes, you can begin to wean yourself from a reliance on established jobs and to find something else to do that is less vulnerable to change. Only by making these mental shifts and beginning to study yourself and your organization with new eyes can you make change work to your advantage.

10: Creating the Transition-worthy Organization

> We're going through a time compression now in our history, in our economy. And what used to take 10 years to evolve has gone to 5, then 4, 3, 2, 1, and now six months. And so the idea of management as some sort of science, with certain principles from which you never deviate, no longer applies. The only practice that's now constant is the practice of constantly accommodating to change—and if you're not changing constantly, you're probably not going to be accommodating to the reality of your world.
>
> William G. McGowan, Chairman,
> MCI Communications Corporation*

In the fall of 1984, *Business Week* carried a cover story that described the difficulties being faced by several of the companies featured in Peters and Waterman's *In Search of Excellence* less than two years after they were presented as examples of "excellence."* Levi Strauss had been caught unprepared when customer tastes changed. Texas Instruments had made an abortive attempt to become a major manufacturer of home computers. And Digital Equipment Corporation, resting on the laurels it had won in the development of minicomputers, had missed significant opportunities as the computer market changed. The title of the article was "Who's Excellent Now?" and the writers clearly felt some satisfaction at having caught Peters and Waterman with their fallibility showing.

These three companies were indeed failing to live up to their touted excellence. But in demonstrating this fact, the *Business Week* writers missed a much larger issue. It was not so much that these companies fell short of the standards that Peters and Waterman had set for them. It was that those hallmarks of excellence had very little to do with the *transition-worthiness* of the organizations being described—and that Levi's and TI and DEC were proving to be very vulnerable indeed to the strains of organizational transition.

Transition-worthiness is an organization's built-in ability to make rapid changes without undue distress and disruption, and it is the life-or-death organizational issue that most of today's management theory skirts. That theory spends more time on where the ship ought to be headed than on how to get the boat there intact. That theory tells about how to sail the organizational boat under normal conditions, when in fact today's storms have torn the sails away and the crew is seasick. And it tells nothing about the seemingly hopeless task of getting somewhere at the same time that you are completely rebuilding the boat.

Although recognizing the need to develop transition-worthiness usually begins with the challenge of managing a particular layoff or a strategic change or a reorganization, transition-worthiness is more than getting through any transition as such. The particular change is a precious opportunity to begin to build in transition-worthiness. That is why the final stage of transition management should always be the review of what happened and the remodeling of the organization's structure, policies, resources, and its very culture to make future transitions easier.

Unfortunately that opportunity is currently being missed by most American companies now suffering through the difficult process of "downsizing." They are still operating as though their particular work-force reduction were a one-time thing, after which regular management practices could be resumed. Very few have recognized that, in MCI's McGowan's words, "the only [management] practice that's now constant is the practice of constantly accommodating to change."

It is easy to see why organizations are so shortsighted. Creating a transition-worthy organization is a large and time-consuming undertaking that itself creates the disruptions and distresses that are typical of all transitions. But unlike most other transitions, this one carries within it its own remedies and leaves the organization better able to weather the future storms of change.

Transition-worthiness requires two qualities. The first is "responsive awareness," which refers to the organization's dynamic and open relation to its changing external environment. The second is "purposeful flexibility," which describes the dynamic organization's ability to reconfigure itself while still remaining purposive.

The idea that an organization ought to be aware and responsive is hardly a new one. It lies behind all the current concern for customer awareness and market-driven strategies—though it is an ideal more often preached than practiced. "A simple summary of what our research uncovered . . . is this," write Peters and Waterman: "the excellent companies *really are* close to their customers. That's it. Other companies talk about it; the excellent companies do it."*

Staying close to customers provides rapid feedback on the changing nature of what they want and how they react to what is offered. But it does more than that. It also provides a way to distinguish between the essential and the incidental in a product or a service. GE's Medical Systems Group provides a good example of this.* In spite of being the world's largest producer of CAT scanners, it had had only modest success in selling them to Japanese hospitals because Toshiba and several European manufacturers could generally underbid its cheapest price of $500,000. The fall in the value of the dollar helped to close the gap, but it was rethinking the product-customer relation that really made the difference. Medical Systems Group's VP Walter L. Robb explains: "In the U.S. you need an opening [in the CAT scanner] that takes bigger people than in Japan, or even Europe. The opening is 70 centimeters, and in Japan, except for sumo wrestlers, nobody is that big. So we made a machine with a 55-centimeter opening, which covers 99% of the people in Japan. It sells as low as $300,000, and we're already getting about a third of our business in Japan in that model."

But listening to the customer, even when practiced as thoughtfully as this, is only part of what is meant by awareness. While it is important to understand the customer's needs and preferences in widgets, it is just as important to know if Korean widgets are about to invade the market, whether OSHA is likely to announce new regulations to protect widget assemblers, how morale is among the widget supervisors, and what new memory chips could mean for widget technology. In other words, awareness depends on being sensitive to everything that could affect the nature, the preparation, or the delivery of the organization's products or services, not just the data that the customer can provide.

Needless to say, being aware of opportunities and dangers means little if the organization cannot respond to them rapidly. Some of the most successful new companies of the past decade have made rapid responsiveness their hallmark. When United Airlines was hamstrung by strikes in 1985, Continental Airlines immediately leased five jets that Braniff was trying to sell, repainted the exteriors, and had them flying newly scheduled flights from Denver within three weeks. More traditional airlines would have taken months to redo the planes, noted an executive from Continental's parent, Texas Air, but the need for quick response outweighed the fact that, as a *Wall Street Journal* reporter said with only a little exaggeration, the paint was still sticky.*

Responsiveness is an important factor in countering overseas competition. In fields as diverse as semiconductors and fashion apparel, it is important to cut down the time it takes to send orders out to suppliers, translate them into manufacturing specifications, ship back the finished products, and market them. Using traditional methods, garments often take more than a year to reach retailers' shelves. Makers like Cherokee have taken business away from overseas manufacturers with an emphasis on faster response—especially to reorders of successful items. The same thing is paying off for a Manteca, California, electronics company, which has undercut overseas suppliers with a ten- instead of a twenty-five-day delivery time on parts.*

Responsive awareness has always been one of the secrets of success in the business world. What is different today is that to a considerable extent responsive awareness is doing what traditional executives have expected planning to do for them. As Peter Drucker has said, today's pace and degree of change means that "no matter how diligent the research, basing a decision on a forecast that goes more than four years into the future is no better than basing it on a coin toss."* Donald Kelly, the CEO of Beatrice Companies, is even more outspoken on the limits of planning today: "Anybody who tells you that he is right where he said he would be two years ago has missed a lot of opportunities along the way."* In such a dynamic environment it has become increasingly critical for the organization to develop an internal and external monitoring system to pick up early signs of change and to develop the technical, structural, and cultural flexibility needed to respond to them.

Computers have made it easier to do some of this monitoring by recording and sorting large amounts of data into reliably comparable categories, so that trends can be spotted more quickly. A San Francisco clothing manufacturer uses computerized inventory management to stay responsive by keeping inventories low, while a Michigan manufacturer of electrical transformers uses computers to track orders and spot unexpected declines early.*

But computers are only an extension of the organization's natural functions of data gathering, sorting, storing, and retrieval. They are part of the organization's "sensory and nervous system." And it is that system, through which the organization picks up signs of approaching change from its environment, that has become critically important today. Everyone in the organization who deals with the external world—from the CEO who lunches with the president of a big account to the person who fields calls at the company switchboard—is part of this sensory system and needs to understand the critical importance of gathering early warnings of change.

Symptoms of inner changes are just as important as those of outer ones. That is why signs of employee distress are so valuable and also so dangerous to overlook. It is, of course, possible to become too preoccupied with them—to become an organizational hypochondriac, as it were. But few organizations today are anywhere close to running that risk. Instead, most of them deny pain, mask it, punish it, and pray that it will pass. Over the years, I've come to regard it as axiomatic that the less a leader or manager will say about the distress being experienced by employees, the more difficulty he or she is going to have with a transition.

I met recently with the director of human resources at a large bank that is widely rumored to be on the verge of taking over a competitor, and I asked him how people in his organization were reacting to the probable acquisition. "I guess some of them are pretty anxious," he said. "They have to realize that if we do that, we'll have to integrate the two staffs, and there won't be room for all of our people." He paused for a moment, then added, "We won't talk about it until the ax actually falls, though." And as our conversation wound down, it became clear that the employees' distress was going to be kept out of everyone's minds until the last possible minute. (His counterpart at the bank that may be acquired, I might add, is far more conscious of the impact of the uncertainty on the staff and the employees and is taking steps to deal openly with it.)

Most leaders and managers rely on their chain of command and their own informal network for internal monitoring, but in a transition-worthy organization something more systematic is needed. The Transition Monitoring Teams described earlier are as useful after a particular change is completed as they are during the change, so it is wise not to disband them when a change is finished. In addition, natural work groups that meet together for general purposes can be educated about transition and what is needed for transition management, so that they can build the monitoring function into their regular meetings as a continuing activity. Their information can be passed on to the Transition Monitoring Team.

In many cases, the problem with organizational awareness comes not from a failure to pick up the information but from a failure to understand its significance—or, worse yet, from a refusal to admit its significance. Here we come to the natural human difficulty with letting go of an old reality, which we discussed back in the chapter on endings. The tactics suggested there will be useful in dealing with misunderstanding and denial, although if the difficulties have been institutionalized as official policy, nothing less than changes in the policy makers themselves will provide the organization with the information it needs to become more transition-worthy.

Some organizations are so resistant to environmental data that doesn't fit the party line that they punish anyone who offers it. For example, Colonel James Burton of the Pentagon's Office of Testing and Evaluation decided to see what would happen if the Army's new Bradley Fighting Vehicle (cost: $2 million each) were hit with a rocket grenade. This might be presumed to be a common battlefield hazard. The Army insisted on scaling down his test to conditions considerably milder ones than those the vehicle might encounter in combat, by removing all ammunition and half the fuel and setting off a charge beside it rather than firing a grenade into it. Even so (in the words of a report on the test) the vehicle "went up like a sky-rocket." The result: The Pentagon went ahead with ordering the new vehicle as planned, and it offered Colonel Burton "a choice of retirement or an assignment in Alaska."*

Lest it seem that I am picking on the military, let it be noted that FMC, Inc., the vehicle's manufacturer, has been sued by an engineer who claims that he was fired because he was so indiscreet as to point out that this supposedly amphibious vehicle had an alarming tendency to sink if struck by waves of more than six inches in height. Although FMC denies the charges, a company document does suggest that the risk of sinking "could be eliminated and a very significant cost saving achieved if the . . . swim requirements [i.e., the requirements that it be able to cross rivers deeper than its height] were deleted."*

Aldous Huxley once suggested that the human brain was best viewed as a reducing valve, cutting down the flow of sensory data so that it came in in quantities that could be assimilated and processed into intelligible patterns. He further suggested that we fail to deal with the full range of "reality" because our brains overdo their job, blocking out too much data and leaving us with a dangerously biased and oversimplified picture of the world. As the Pentagon and FMC illustrate, the organizational brain does the same thing. But the implications of the tendency go beyond the usual government boondoggle. For in the end the organization itself suffers, because the information that is needed to deal successfully with a changing environment is too often blocked out before it can be received.

There are two main ways to deal with this difficulty. The first is to track back along the information routes and find who is screening out the inadmissible data. (It may, of course, be the leader who is the culprit, but whoever it is has to understand the seriously crippling effect of the practice . . . and stop it.) The second way is for executives themselves to get out and spend more time at the interface between the organization and the external world. They need to recognize that their external function is not just to promote the organization, but to learn on its behalf. Few leaders spend much time as learners, which is too bad, since you cannot respond to what you do not know or understand. As Harry Levinson has written, "Responsiveness to the environment and to the changes taking place around an organization is probably the most fundamental requirement of leadership."*

Responsiveness presumes the ability to regroup internally to take advantage of an opportunity or forestall a danger. So organizational *flexibility* is the other side of the transition-worthiness equation, and it is important in an environment where reliable long-range planning is difficult for the same reasons that responsiveness is. CEO Graham Briggs, of Charles River Data Systems Inc., has put it well: ". . . flexibility can be an awfully good substitute for foresight."*

There is today a great deal of talk about "trimming the fat" from our organizations and about getting "lean," but I suspect this may have more to do with our preoccupation with thinness than it does with organizational effectiveness. In attempting to work off their "middle management bulge," many organizations are swinging to the other extreme of organizational anorexia, as their work-force reductions leave them so understaffed that they can no longer adequately perform their basic functions—much less those functions *plus* the task of creating a new and different organization. Leanness may be the hallmark of a good steak, but flexibility is a more important organizational quality. As Rosabeth Moss Kanter says, "In an innovating organization . . . security will come not from domination but from flexibility. It will come not from having everything under control, but from quick reaction time [and] being able to cut across categories to get the best combinations of people for the job."*

Building more flexibility into an organization may involve changing the production system technically, procuring more items and services from other organizations, shrinking inventories and developing ways to replenish them quickly, using temporary workers, and developing special project teams. Those changes need to be accompanied by a whole range of changes on a less visible level, so that the policies, procedures, systems, and the organization's culture itself support the changes.

Taken singly, the many different strategies for increasing flexibility are being widely preached and increasingly practiced by American organizations. Computer-integrated manufacturing and just-in-time inventorying are examples, but they are usually undertaken as solutions to cost or quality problems rather than as elements in a systematic program of building flexibility into the organization. What is missing is the larger context of transition-worthiness as an organizational goal. That is a serious oversight, for the greatest value of computer-integrated manufacturing and just-in-time inventorying is that they increase the organization's ability to change direction fast without upsetting everyone.

Companies of all sizes are discovering in automated manufacturing processes not only an answer to the competition from low-wage overseas manufacturers, but also a way to transform the production process into something flexible enough to respond quickly to the different needs of particular customers. Frost Inc., of Grand Rapids, Michigan, was a one-product company that built the overhead trolley mechanisms used by American auto makers to pull cars down the assembly line.* Detroit's hard times nearly wiped Frost out, and owner-manager Chad Frost tried to diversify. "Every time we'd try to make a new product, we screwed up," he told a *Wall Street Journal* reporter. "The fundamental problem was inflexibility. We had single-purpose machines and single-purpose people."

So in the fall of 1983 he launched a major program to develop that flexibility through automating "everything from the front office to the factory floor, with personal computers, industrial robots, computer-controlled machine tools and a computer-directed monorail that delivers materials and finished goods where needed." The renovation of the company—which included a shift in management style as well as technology—is not quite complete, but already sales per employee have doubled, to over $150,000. Almost half of the $15 million in annual revenues comes from custom-made products that would have been impossible for the inflexible company of three years ago to make.

Milwaukee-based Allen-Bradley has gone even further in the relay and contacter assembly line called Department 260.* There, orders as small as a single item can be customized without losing mass-production speed. With the help of the kinds of bar codes that supermarkets use to price products, Allen-Bradley engineers developed a way for a string of orders for different versions of their products to be translated into instructions for the machinery. When the code gives it the signal, for example, a screwdriver assembly moves upward and inserts a larger screw farther up on the frame, because it is a larger contacter frame that is being assembled. But then the next code, for a smaller frame, will signal the assembly to insert a smaller screw in a lower position. Such changes go on constantly, allowing the assembly line to turn out any combination of the six hundred different varieties of the electrical components that are made in Department 260.

The promise of such automation is still far from fully realized, but it represents a huge reversal of the movement toward inflexibility that mass production has entailed during the past century. In clothing, for example, clothing sizes were not standardized until the Civil War, but in only a few years that standardization permitted machines to cut and sew clothing. It turned custom-made clothing into a handmade specialty item for the wealthy. But with computer-integrated manufacturing it is now quite possible to translate an order for a one-of-a-kind garment into instructions to an automated production line that presents the right fabric to a laser cutter, which cuts a perfect design pattern and size and transfers it to automated sewing machines for assembly. The machine-made results can be worn by a customer before a similar product made by overseas handworkers or domestic seamstresses could even be finished.

Technological flexibility must be matched by flexibility in the work force. One answer lies in the increasing use of temporary workers, not only in the time-honored situations where a clerk or secretary is sick or on vacation, but for much longer periods and for everything from computer programmers to lawyers to accountants. You can even get a doctor for your company clinic or a chief financial officer to handle finances for a while in a new subsidiary. In San Francisco, a company called The Corporate Staff can rent you the services of a hundred general management executives, and its business has tripled within the past year.*

Pitney Bowes, Inc., of Stamford, Connecticut, usually has more than 50 temporary engineers working there, and corporate purchasing administrator Robert Bryson explains why: "It's a very easy way to scale up and down for engineering projects." The alternatives involve hiring and layoffs, which are both expensive and traumatic. Some companies build temporaries into their long-term plans. Hospital Corporation of America is planning to lease 120 workers in a new psychiatric facility it is building in California. About 30 percent of Motorola Inc.'s work force of *90,000* are temporary employees who can be laid off within twenty-four hours, and another 40 percent work on six-month contracts.

Both automation and the use of temporaries have their own pitfalls, of course, for each of them is sure to require more far-reaching organizational changes if it is to work. Automated manufacturing, according to one expert, "cannot be implemented effectively within existing organizations." The same thing is true of using temps to acquire greater responsiveness and flexibility. As the organization shifts from using temporaries as short-term replacements to using them as what is beginning to be called a "contingent" work force to staff projects on an indeterminate basis, the permanent workers are likely to feel threatened. In response, there needs to be not only skillful transition management when the composition of the work force changes, but also a redefinition of employment security if this resistance is to be softened. By guaranteeing employment to its permanent core of workers, the organization can expand and contract around its periphery without fearing that flexibility will turn into chaos. Motorola, for example, guarantees employment to the 30 percent of its employees who have been there at least ten years.*

Change being what it is, employment security requires a further change, and that is developing the capacity to dissolve and re-form work teams as the need arises.* A recent study of IBM's dominance in its field concludes that it came about not because of superior technology, skillful marketing, innovative products, or intelligent leadership. It came about, argues Brian Jeffery in a *Datamation* article, because "IBM is uncommonly good at . . . shuffling its organizational structure around to deploy management, capital, and technical resources to exploit an opportunity or address a problem."

The core of IBM's genius for reorganization is what Jeffery calls its "modularity." IBM has, he writes, "a bedrock of product units . . . and geographically based marketing and administrative units. These provide clusters of expertise and form the basic building blocks of the organization. They can be combined into divisions, and divisions combined into groups, according to the needs of the moment." This combination and recombination goes on constantly to meet emerging needs. The company moves in quickly "when the initial goals have been achieved and . . . the organization is dismantled and assigned to new structure and new management."

The transitions required by such changes would have long since ripped the company apart were it not for an infrastructure of support systems and retraining programs to help employees shift from old tasks and old identities to new ones. In 1985 the company retrained 10,000 workers for new jobs and helped some 3,500 of them (to the tune of $60,000 each) to change locations to take those jobs. IBM provides the resources necessary to support people in transition, and any organization that recognizes that transition-worthiness is necessary for survival must do the same.

IBM's transition-worthiness was tested in 1982 when the recession and an influx of Japanese 64K memory chips cut the sales of products from the Burlington, Vermont, semiconductor plant. Instead of closing the plant or laying off the workers, the company decided to develop and retrain workers to produce a 256K chip. To lower the cost of the new product, they reorganized the whole factory. And they took the following steps to avoid the layoffs that other computer firms were going through:

1. They cut out overtime.

2. They encouraged workers to take unpaid leaves of absence if they had any reason to do so.

3. They transferred some manufacturing workers to research to speed up the development of the new chip.

4. They cut out one hundred student jobs.

5. They let temps go.

6. Some subcontracted work was brought back inhouse and given to idle IBM workers.

7. A team was formed to look for positions at other IBM facilities for excess nonmanufacturing employees.

8. When sales picked up, some nonmanufacturing employees were retrained as manufacturing employees, with the promise that they could return to their nonmanufacturing positions in a year.

9. A generous early-retirement program was instituted, and some people in their fifties, who would not otherwise have been able to do so, retired.

As of 1985 and after three years in which semiconductor jobs in America were disappearing by the tens of thousands, no one at the Burlington plant had lost his or her job. In 1986, buffeted by further difficulties, IBM finally broke with its long-standing policy of not laying off regular full-time workers. But the exception simply illustrated the strength of the rule, for the layoffs were clearly a last resort, and IBM workers continue to be more secure in their employment than are the workers for IBM's competitors.

There is a large fly in this particular ointment, however. Security for IBM workers has meant insecurity for many of its subcontractors' employees. As production at the Burlington plant dwindled and subcontracted parts were no longer contracted out, people at small supplier companies had to be laid off. That outcome illustrates a problem that must be faced by any organization seeking to create transition-worthiness: a review of its market to discover ways of reducing the organization's vulnerability to the kinds of reversals suffered by anyone dependent on one big customer or a cluster of customers that are likely to act en masse.

IBM's subs provide an instructive example of the strategies that vulnerable companies can use. A recent *Wall Street Journal* article reviewed some of the ways that such companies are buffering their dependence on a giant.* Some, such as Soft-Switch, Inc., and Artificial Intelligence Corp., are openly courting IBM's competitors as well as IBM. Others, such as Tricom Automotive Data Systems Inc. and Software Publishing Corp., are signing nonexclusive marketing contracts with IBM to avoid the danger of total dependence. Most important, many companies, such as Vermont Microsystems, have persuaded IBM to make unusually large production commitments, to underwrite speculative design contracts, and sometimes even to guarantee a minimum profit on sales. The details are specific to this particular market, but the general strategies are adaptable to any situation in which market dependency locks an organization into a dangerous inflexibility.

The cancellation of orders by one's main customer is only one of a number of crises that can befall a company. An integral part of creating the transition-worthy organization is developing crisis-management scenarios in advance. Without a plan, an organization can be permanently damaged before it has any time to adapt. In some organizations any attempt to foresee possible disasters is considered a sign of negativity or even disloyalty. But it is neither. Rather it is an essential part of creating transition-worthiness.

A crisis-management plan must take account of three different kinds of crises. The first is intrinsic to the organization's operation, the kinds of risks it runs just being staffed by fallible human beings while it does whatever it does. The oil spill, the banker who embezzles, and the tainted shipment of canned food are examples of this kind of crisis. Any organization that lacks plans for such eventualities has an attitude toward survival that is reckless, if not suicidal. The second crisis comes when a plan fails or has to be aborted. There may have been no way to foresee the failure, but any good planning effort—especially one based on some kind of forecast—must have built-in alternative strategies if things do not turn out as planned. A plan without a section on contingencies is a winner-take-all gamble. The third type of crisis is extrinsic to the organization: a tornado hits the warehouse, the CEO's plane goes down, the supplier of a key raw material suddenly triples its price. Here the possibilities are endless and, to some extent, unforeseeable. But a generic crisis-management plan must be created:

1. Who is responsible for the first round of decisions—and who else if that person isn't available?

2. How will immediate fact-finding be carried out?

3. What are the basic policies governing the release of information; i.e., how honest do we intend to be?

4. How will employees be kept informed?

5. Who will the spokesperson be for public information, and who for employee communications?

6. Who needs to make the decisions after those made on the spot —who needs to agree to them and who else needs to be kept informed?

Needless to say, crisis management must presume that everything possible is done in advance to keep crises from happening. By contingency planning, the flexible organization builds its readiness for the unexpected, and by remedial action the responsive organization deals with potential dangers before they can cause real trouble.

There is one kind of "crisis" that is so foreseeable that it is a wonder that all organizations do not have plans on how to deal with it. That is the crisis that occurs when a product or service is rendered obsolete by changes in technique or design. Such an outcome is a natural part of the product life cycle, and it is also inherent in the life cycle of those structures and strategies developed to support the product and the part of the organization that supplies it. The organization must prepare itself by working out in advance the way that the product or process will be phased out and the way that a replacement for it will be developed.

But if it seems that organizations should naturally make such plans, it is also not so hard to see why they do not. To do so is to question the very basis on which the organization's security rests. As Richard Foster has recently argued in *Innovation: The Attacker's Advantage,* it is especially hard for a successful organization to abandon the very things on which its success has been based. The more successful the organization, the harder it is to let go of what got it there. That is the natural advantage that the small and not-yet-successful organization has. With less of its identity tied up in an established line of products and services, it can afford to be more flexible.

Such life-cycle planning has some significant cultural implications, for the leadership of the organization must have or develop the ability to think in cyclical rather than linear terms. This involves:

1. A shift away from thinking of growth mechanically to ways of thinking organically—toward thinking of the ultimate demise of any form of output as natural and foreseeable. Only in that way can one capitalize on the potentialities of the full life cycle of a system or a service rather than viewing its life as a period of things going well, followed by a period of things going badly—a success, followed by a failure.

2. Developing the habit of thinking what could replace the outlived product or process while that element is still in the prime of its organizational life. This goes beyond general R&D to the question "What's going to take the place of X?"

3. Using the existing entity in the later stages of its cycle as a way of subsidizing operations while a new entity is being developed.

4. Teaching everyone a new way of looking at endings, in which they are the natural conclusions of a life cycle rather than the signs of failure.

5. Revising promotion and incentives policies, so that they reward life-cycle management and not just linear "success." It must be as valuable to a manager's career to oversee the orderly aging and termination of a product or service as it is valuable to the organization to have it managed well.

Lacking these things, organizations avoid the task of planning and managing endings. The result is, in Peter Drucker's words, that "far too few businesses are willing to slough off yesterday, and as a result, far too few have resources available for tomorrow."*

Being ready to abandon yesterday's arrangements will fail if it is seen as a way of abandoning yesterday's people, so this kind of flexibility must be accompanied by a commitment to help those people get ready for tomorrow. That commitment must be evident in several forms:

1. A stated employment security policy.

2. An "inplacement" system, through which employees who belong to groups that are being phased out are relocated in groups that have a future. This is more than an inhouse placement service, for like the outplacement programs which it parallels, it must begin with an opportunity for the employees to reassess their goals and abilities so that every relocation is a chance for a better fit between the personal nature and the organizational need. And it must be based on the kind of strategies for capitalizing on change that were described in the previous chapter.

3. Well-designed ability-identification and performance-appraisal systems to provide management with the information it needs to manage human resources wisely—and an organizational commitment to use them. (As the human resources vice-president of a large chemical company told me recently, "We know how to separate the wheat from the chaff—we just don't do it!")

4. Retraining programs to prepare employees technically for new roles and the interpersonal skills that they require. These programs will be much easier to operate and the disruptiveness of transition will be minimized if there is considerable cross-training going on all the time.

5. A willingness to build a little slack into the staffing of the organization, so that, in small numbers, people can actually be spared for such cross-training and retraining.

6. Incentives for making transitions. The incentive system, like the promotion system, is often based on the linear image of onward-and-upward, rather than on the cyclical image of seasonal change. The flexible organization will need to reward its people for helping with the common business of transitions, not just for the private business of getting ahead.

Along with these outward manifestations, there must be an underlying ethic of responsibility. "Organizational ethics" are usually thought to involve the avoidance of dishonest or destructive acts: overcharging, misinformation, damage to the environment, etc. But the largest ethical issue faced by today's organizations is not likely to show up on that list, no matter how long it is. That issue is the ethical implication of how the organization handles the changes that it causes. Most organizations currently make changes with little regard for their impact, inside the organization or outside. But that is a luxury that was affordable only in a constantly expanding economy.

Today, the constant shifts, cutbacks, and expansions are whipping people around in a way that is destroying not only their loyalty to their organizations but their self-confidence, their spirit, and their concern for others as well. A whole society of such people would be an awful prospect, and we are well on our way toward creating such a society. It is the ethical responsibility of our organizations to do what they can to reverse that trend. It is also sensible to do so because an organization made up of such people will be simply too unstable to survive in the long run. But to say that it is good business to take care of people in times of rapid change must not make us forget that it is also and more fundamentally a question of ethics, of the values that give us our self-respect, and of our sense that we are helping to build and not tear down a society.

As the organization moves toward greater transition-worthiness, it must also utilize the classical stuff of culture: the folklore, the ritual, and the symbolism that convey the new goals and priorities of an organization and make them memorable. The folklore takes the form of the stories that are told about the organization and its history. It matters little whether the stories are "true" in a literal sense, only that they are "true to life" and express something significant about how the organization does things.

A team of researchers from the Stanford Business School has studied the stories being told at dozens of companies and businesses and has decided that they fall into seven categories which can be summarized thus:

1. Does everyone follow the rules?
2. How can power-holders be expected to behave?
3. Can a person progress upward through the company?
4. Does the company take care of its own during hard times?
5. Does the company take care of its own when they have to move?
6. How are mistakes dealt with by superiors?
7. How will the organization deal with obstacles?*

Compare, for example the following two stories recorded in two comparable companies with quite different cultures. One company's story dealt with the time when competitors were laying off employees, while at that company everyone including the president took a 10 percent cut in pay and worked only nine days in every ten. The story at the other company was that a brand-new manager was instructed by his superior to lay off forty people that day. "By the way," he was told, "we quit here at five-fifteen, so don't notify anybody until five o'clock. We want a full day's work out of them." While leaders and managers cannot implant a story that does not fit the culture—it just won't be remembered and retold—they can look for and talk about incidents that express the new shape that things are taking. Research on the subject makes it clear that, to a degree surprising to literal-minded people, illustrative stories are more likely to be remembered, to generate belief, and to encourage commitment than statistical data that "proves" the point in a factual way.

Ritual too should be used to dramatize transition-worthiness. Leaders have always been sensitive to its power, but organizational theory has been slow to recognize its significance. Donald Clifford, the author of *The Winning Performance,* describes a restructuring that involved difficult demotions, where ritual was used effectively:

> One company moved a whole layer of senior managers [who were not performing well in a changed business environment] down to lower-level jobs, which they could perform with excellence, gave them comfortable offices and celebrated the occasion with a dinner dance at an excellent hotel. At this event the fine past performances of these managers were remembered in a series of speeches that were genuine and warm. The downward transition was a success for the individuals and the company.*

Visual and verbal symbolism are likewise useful in bringing a change into focus and summarizing it. That is why new companies name themselves so carefully—or, in the case of United States Steel, International Harvester, and 1,380 other companies, renamed themselves in 1986. That is why logos are so significant. That is why the fact that there is (or is not) a company jet has an importance that is much more than economic and practical. That is why one company encourages its people to wear white shirts and dark ties and another encourages sports shirts and jeans—and why both of them may change their dress codes if the companies begin to change their styles of management.

Important though the organizational culture is and powerful though an organization's leadership can be in conveying symbolic messages about the end of one era and the beginning of a new one, there are some things that need to be done on such a large scale that they cannot be done entirely by the company itself. These are things that investors and union leaders and legislators must consider doing if we are to create an environment that encourages the rise of transition-worthy organizations in the future.

The mood of impatience among today's investors seriously inhibits the organizational reorientations that will be necessary if today's companies are to be viable tomorrow. Demands for quick return on investments discourage long-range strategies required by life-cycle planning. As economist Lester Thurow of MIT has written, "Any elementary economic textbook will tell you that finance exists to serve industry; now we're busy making industry into a plaything for finance."*

Union rules about who can do what work and how many of them it takes to do it discourage the internal flexibility that management must have if it is to orchestrate successful transitions and avoid the yo-yo reversals of laying off and rehiring its permanent workers. Such flexibility is far more effective in putting American industry back into the running with the foreign competition than is the more visible issue of wages. As an Arthur Young & Co. consultant said recently, "Unfortunately you can still find managements that spend all the time . . . getting more wage concessions when their labor cost is already down to only 10 percent of the cost of goods sold."

Many legislative programs need to be rewritten. Right to Work and Fair Employment Practices laws need to be revised so that companies are encouraged to protect the employees who are with them for the long haul and are not so vulnerable to wrongful discharge suits that are based on technical infractions and the capricious results of court cases. Corporate tax laws need to be changed to encourage companies to retain and reinvest earnings instead of paying them out to impatient investors. And legal protections must be built to make such a fund of retained earnings safe from corporate raiders. While some corporate takeovers certainly benefit everyone, the only sure way to avoid the damaging ones is to develop the kinds of rigidities and liabilities that discourage any takeover bid— and, incidentally, leave the organization far less transition-worthy than it was before. Deregulation itself needs to be reconsidered. In some areas, like airlines, it has not served either consumers or most of the businesses themselves. The issue there is, once again, that rapid changes are whipping companies back and forth so that many of them are coming apart.

The government also needs to help the corporate world create an employee benefit system that transcends the boundaries of individual organizations. We badly need what a *Business Week* editorial recently called "portable benefits" that can be protected and will continue to accrue when an employee changes employers.* Such benefits would make the mobility that so clearly lies ahead of us far less painful.

In short, there has to be a greatly increased public awareness of what needs to be done to create organizations that can survive longer than a few years. That will come about only as a result of organizational leaders articulating those needs in a systematic, not piecemeal, fashion. It is the systematic overview of these needs that will also help to sort out the essential and functional needs from those that are special and self-serving.

I don't want to end this book on managing organizational transition with recommendations about what the government ought to do, for even if the government does these things, the final burden of transition management must fall on the shoulders of the leaders of the organizations themselves. Leaders of transition-worthy organizations are going to have to meet the challenge of change with a new outlook and are going to have to build that outlook into a new set of cultural norms within their organizations. The shift to these new norms can be captured in what might be called "The Ten C's" of an organization culture that is transition-worthy:

Change: No longer viewed as an exception, but rather as the rule.

Challenge: No longer signaling the need for survival behavior, but signaling the need for learning behavior.

Control: No longer referring to keeping everything in place, but rather to keeping things in rhythm and balance.

Chaos: No longer experienced as meaningless confusion, but rather as the sign of the neutral zone and as energy waiting to be reintegrated into new form.

Creativity: No longer a special response to special cases, but rather the essential, normal response to transition.

Confidence: No longer based on knowing what exactly you are doing, but rather on your ability to deal with ambiguity and the unknown.

Commitment: No longer defined as an allegiance to an established status quo, but rather as loyalty to common underlying interests that are best served by a continually changing pattern of organizational arrangements.

Community: No longer made up of those close by, but rather of those in one's network.

Choice: No longer simply selecting the preferable, but rather affirming and looking for meaning in the actual.

Career: No longer a trip, but rather a journey.

A journey has been defined as a trip in which the luggage has been lost. Markets that only a decade ago were completely secure are being lost. Jobs that led somewhere when we took them now lead nowhere. Yesterday's plans, organizational and personal alike, are having to be abandoned. This is not happening just in America. Even Japan, with its celebrated tradition of lifetime employment, is beginning to feel the losses that come with rapid change. Three new outplacement agencies have recently been set up to deal with the increase in *kata-takaki,* or "tapping on the shoulder" to inform an employee that he or she is being terminated. Perhaps America's is not so much a declining economy as simply the first economy to enter the twenty-first century.

But not all the change, here or elsewhere, is decline. New plans are being made. New companies are springing up around the rubble of the old like new shoots around old stumps. New management strategies are being formulated to capitalize on today's opportunities. Everywhere change is challenging the skill and the understanding of individuals and organizations. Today, we are indeed on a journey—the trip is over. And whatever the destination, getting there requires managing transition successfully.

NOTES

INTRODUCTION

Pages ix–x: Information about the Colt .45, from Eduardo Lachica, "The Cavalry Is Gone; Now Will the Army Get Rid of the Colts?" *The Wall Street Journal,* June 20, 1984, p. 1.

CHAPTER ONE

Page 3: The first epigraph is quoted in "Airlines in Flux: And Then There Were Five?" *Business Week,* March 10, 1986, p. 107.

Page 6: On Quality Control, see Jeremy Main, "Under the Spell of the Quality Gurus." *Fortune,* August 18, 1986, p. 34.

Page 8: The vignette about the Crocker and Wells Fargo employees was reported by columnist Herb Caen, San Francisco *Chronicle,* February 11, 1986, p. 28.

Page 8: The statistics on the Gulf and Beatrice mergers are from Paul Farhi, "New Faces Won't Bring Big Change at 'Gray' Chevron," San Francisco *Examiner,* January 5, 1986, p. D2, and Thomas F. O'Boyle, "Loyalty Ebbs at Many Companies as Employees Grow Disillusioned," *The Wall Street Journal,* July 11, 1985, p. 29.

Page 9: Sigler's comment on "the people trauma" is in Stephen F. Prokeach, "People Traumas in Mergers," New York *Times,* November 19, 1985, p. D1.

Page 10: The Tocqueville quote is from G. W. Pierson, *Tocqueville and Beaumont in America* (New York: Oxford University Press, 1938), p. 119.

Pages 11–12: Information about McGraw-Hill is given by Stuart Gannes, "Marketing Is the Message at McGraw-Hill," *Fortune,* February 17, 1986, p. 35.

Page 13: Sanko's experience is described in Joshua Hyatt, "When Parent Companies Create Orphans, *Inc.,* October 1985, p. 20.

Page 13: See William J. Abernathy, Kim B. Clark, and Alan M. Kantrow, *Industrial Renaissance* (New York: Basic Books, 1983), p. 123.

Page 14: The Opinion Research data is given in Thomas O'Boyle, "Loyalty Ebbs . . ." During the same period, favorable ratings given by clerical workers dropped from 52 percent to 37 percent and by hourlies from 36 percent to 21 percent.

Page 14: Statistics on cases from Joy Zimmerman, "Job Related Stress," *Pacific Sun,* November 15, 1985, pp. 8–11.

Page 15: Quotation from Donald Schon, *Beyond the Stable State* (New York: Random House, 1971), p. 163.

Page 16: Harry Levinson was quoted in "The Business Gurus," San Francisco *Chronicle,* December 2, 1985, p. 25.

CHAPTER TWO

Pages 17 ff: For a full-scale study of the transition process in the individual life, see my book *Transitions: Making Sense of Life's Changes* (Reading, Massachusetts: Addison-Wesley Publishing Co., 1980).

Page 17: See "Macy's Tough Battle to Stay on Top," San Francisco *Chronicle,* December 15, 1986, p. 19.

Pages 19 ff: Xerox's experience is described in Dexter Hutchins, "Having a Hard Time with Just in Time," *Fortune,* June 18, 1986, pp. 64–66.

Page 22: The Galsworthy quote is from his *Over the River* (London: William Heineman, 1933), p. 4.

Pages 22–23: The example of where Pasteur's work with infectious diseases began is taken from Arthur Koestler, *The Act of Creation,* (New York: The Macmillan Company, 1964), p. 193.

Page 23: On the inventor of Novocaine, see Peter Drucker, *Innovation and Entrepreneurship* (New York: Harper and Row, 1985), pp. 190–91.

Page 28: On typology, see Carl Jung, *Psychological Types,* Vol. 6 of *The Collected Works* (New York: Pantheon Books, 1953).

Pages 28–29: For male/female differences, see Carol Gilligan, *In a Different Voice* (Cambridge, Massachusetts: Harvard University Press, 1982).

Page 29: For theories of life's natural phases, see "A Lifetime of Transitions" in my book *Transitions,* pp. 27–56. See also "The Life Cycle: Epigenesis of Identity," in Erik H. Erikson, *Identity, Youth, and Crisis* (New York: W. W. Norton & Co., 1968), pp. 91–141; Roger L. Gould, M.D., *Transformations: Growth and Change in Adult Life* (New York: Simon & Schuster, 1978); and Daniel J. Levinson et al., *The Seasons of a Man's Life* (New York: Alfred A. Knopf, 1978).

Page 30: James and Elizabeth Bugental, "A Fate Worse Than Death: The Fear of Changing," *Psychotheraphy,* 21:4 (1984), pp. 543–49.

Pages 31–32: The contrast with the Japanese is made by Richard T. Pascale and Anthony G. Athos in *The Art of Japanese Management* (New York: Simon & Schuster, 1981), pp. 92–93.

CHAPTER THREE

Page 37: The story of disillusioned Nobel winners was part of an Associated Press article, appearing in the Santa Rosa, California, *Press Democrat,* December 9, 1984, p. 13C. The research on life change events was originally published in *The Journal of Psychosomatic Medicine,* 11 (1967), pp. 213–18. It has been reprinted in many places, including newspaper and magazine articles, and in a pamphlet called *Stress* (Chicago: Blue Cross Association, 1974).

Page 39: Peter Marris, *Loss and Change* (New York: Pantheon Books, 1974), p. 99.

Page 39: The essay with the AT&T quote is in Ralph H. Kilmann et al., eds., *Gaining Control of the Corporate Culture* (San Francisco: Jossey Bass, 1985), p. 59.

Page 40. "Attachment" as a concept and a great deal of valuable commentary on the impact of its loss is contained in John Bowlby, *Loss: Sadness and Depression,* which is Vol. III of *Attachment and Loss* (New York: Basic Books, Inc., 1980).

Page 41. The description of the plant-closing ceremony is from a personal communication by one of the consultants who worked with plant personnel on the closure, Jane B. Russell.

Page 42. The example of automation giving managers new information is from Edgar H. Schein, "How Culture Forms, Develops, and Changes," in Kilmann, et al., eds., op. cit., p. 18.

Pages 42–43. The data on relocation is in "Planning a Move," *Venture,* June 1985, p. 33.

Page 43. For a good brief introduction to the art of negotiation, see Roger Fisher, *Getting to YES: The Strategy of Successful Negotiation* (Boston, Massachusetts: Houghton Mifflin, 1981).

Page 44. The profile of Walter Bauer is in Cheryl Crooks, "After the Axe," *California Business,* July 1986, p. 54.

Page 46. The Exxon employee is quoted in "The End of Corporate Loyalty," *Business Week,* August 4, 1986, p. 48.

Page 49: Shelley E. Taylor, "Adjustment to Threatening Events: A Theory of Cognitive Adaptation," *American Psychologist,* November 1983, pp. 1161–73.

Pages 49–50. Many of these examples of loss of faith come from N. R. Kleinfield's article, "Company Scandals," in *International Herald Tribune,* July 17, 1985, p. 6. The quote from Robins's Robert Watts is from a *Wall Street Journal* article on the company's troubles (December 15, 1986, p. 12).

Page 52. The Marris quotation is from, *Change and Loss,* pp. 91 and 103.

Pages 53ff. *Loss,* p. 85. Bowlby is discussing bereavement in his book, although he sometimes draws parallels to other losses that make it clear that the same basic patterns apply in any significant, identity-threatening loss.

Page 54. On bargaining, see *On Death and Dying* (New York: Macmillan Publishing Co., 1969).

Page 57. Terrence E. Deal, "Cultural Change: Opportunity, Silent Killer, or Metamorphosis," in Ralph H. Kilmann et al., eds., *Gaining Control of the Corporate Culture* (San Francisco: Jossey-Bass, 1985), p. 293.

Page 58. Oz Hopkins, "Stress Related Ailments Linked to Mt. St. Helens," *The Oregonian,* May 16, 1985, p. B2. See also Kai Erikson's study of a dam breaking: *Everything in Its Path* (New York: Simon & Schuster, 1976).

CHAPTER FOUR

Page 59. The epigraphs are from Rollo May, *The Courage to Create* (New York: Bantam Books, 1976), pp. 66–67 and *Selections from the Prison Notebooks of Antonio Gramsci,* ed. Quinten Hoare and Geoffrey Nowell-Smith (London: Lawrence & Wishart, 1971).

Page 60. The statistic on terrorist acts comes from "Profiting from Perilous Times," *Money* (June 1986), p. 27.

Page 64. Roger Smith's comment about the changes at GM came from a *Wall Street Journal* report on the changes that appeared on the front page of that paper on March 14, 1985.

Page 69. On rites of passage, see Arnold van Gennep, *Rites of Passage,* trans. Monika B. Vizedon and Gabrielle Caffee (Chicago: University of Chicago Press, 1960) and Mircea Eliade, *Myths, Dreams, and Mysteries,* trans. Philip Mairet (New York: Harper & Row, 1960).

Pages 69–70. John Bowlby, *Loss: Sadness and Depression,* Vol. III of *Attachment and Loss* (New York: Basic Books, Inc., 1980), p. 122 and 246.

Page 72. Kanter's comments are on pp. 96–97 of *The Change Masters* (New York: Simon & Schuster, 1985).

Pages 72ff. *A Study of History* (Abridgment of Vols. I–VI by D. C. Somervell) (New York: Oxford University Press, 1947), p. 217.

Page 73. Edward deBono, *Lateral Thinking for Management* (New York: Penguin, 1982).

Pages 74–75. Turner's original list is in *The Ritual Process* (Chicago: Aldine Publishing Co., 1969), p. 106.

Pages 76–77. "Disaster-Relief Expert Believes in Self-Help Instead of Handouts," *The Wall Street Journal,* December 17, 1986, p. 1.

CHAPTER FIVE

Pages 79ff. The information on Pacific Mutual is taken from company publications, interviews with several of its vice-presidents, and Trevor Bailey's article "No Small Change for Walter Gerken," *AirCal Magazine,* March 1986, pp. 23–28.

Page 82. Charles Lofy is a psychologist at Mankato State University, Minnesota. He is one of the few people to have used our transition model to work with people dealing with social change.

Page 88. The analogy of the landscape architect is taken from an article on reorganization called "Tracks in the Snow" by a Canadian consultant named Gary Robinson. The article appeared in the *ODN Newsletter,* Winter, 1986, pp. 7–8.

Page 90. Context-based training is discussed by Marty Lefkoe in "Shifting Context: A Better Approach to Training?" in *Training* (February 1985, pp. 43–47).

Pages 92ff. On the use of ritual, see Harrison M. Trice and Janice M. Beyer, "Using Six Organizational Rites to Change Culture" in Ralph H. Kilman et al., eds., *Gaining Control of the Corporate Culture* (San Francisco: Jossey Bass, 1985), pp. 370–99 and "Rites and Rituals," Chapter 4 of *Corporate Cultures* by Terrence E. Deal and Allan A. Kennedy (Reading, Massachusetts: Addison-Wesley, 1982).

Pages 95ff. On breaking a large beginning down into small steps, see Karl E. Weick in "Small Wins: Redefining the Scale of Social Problems," *The American Psychologist,* January 1984. The Peters quote is from the same essay.

CHAPTER SIX

Page 97. The Adizes article appeared in *Organizational Dynamics* Summer, 1979, pp. 3–25.

Pages 98ff. The life cycle here presented draws on the work of Adizes and that of other organizational theorists. See also Neil C. Churchill and Virginia L. Lewis, "The Five Stages of Small Business Growth," *Harvard Business Review* (May–June 1983), pp. 30–50, and Thomas A. McCauley and John Moore, "Design for Living," *Management Focus* (September–October 1984), pp. 22–28.

Page 106. On Ovshinsky's role at ECD, see "How to Succeed in Business Without Really Selling," *Business Week,* May 19, 1986.

Pages 109–110. The story of Sims and Continuous Aim Firing is taken from Elting Morison's article, "Gunfire at Sea: Conflict Over a New Technology," *Engineering and Science* (April 1950).

Pages 112ff. Abernathy, Clark, and Kantrow have discussed the Rejuvenation process under the unfortunate label of "de-maturity" in their *Industrial Renaissance,* (New York: Basic Books, 1983).

Page 113. For examples of Rejuvenation, see Joel Kotkin, "The Revenge of the Fortune 500," *Inc.,* August 1985, pp. 39–44; "New Rx for Ailing Hospitals, San Francisco *Chronicle,* August, 18, 1986, pp. 19, 22; and two *Business Week* articles, "Can Jack Welch Reinvent GE (June 30, 1986) and "Dow Chemical's Drive to Change its Market—and Its Image (June 9, 1986).

Page 114. *The Seasons of a Man's Life* (New York: Alfred A. Knopf, 1978), p. 212.

Pages 115ff. McGowan's statements are from an interview in *Inc.,* August 1986, pp. 29–38.

CHAPTER SEVEN

Page 119. See James MacGregor Burns, *Leadership* (New York: Harper and Row, 1978).

Pages 121–122. The profile of Burr is "Bitter Victories," *Inc.,* August 1985, pp. 25–35.

Page 124. The comment on the papacy is made by Harry Levinson in *Executive* (Cambridge, Massachusetts: Harvard University Press, 1981).

Pages 125ff. These descriptions of the four basic types are drawn from a number of sources, especially Humphrey Osmond, Miriam Siegler, and Richard Smoke, "Typology Revisited: A New Perspective," *Psychological Perspectives,* Fall, 1977, pp. 206–19; David Keirsey and Marilyn Bates, *Please Understand Me: Character & Temperament Types,* 3rd Ed. (Del Mar, California: Prometheus Nemesis, 1978), pp. 27–66 and 129–165; and Isabel Briggs Myers, *Gifts Differing* (Palo Alto, California: Consulting Psychologists Press, 1980), pp. 4–7.

Pages 127ff. Most of the material on Debbi Fields (and her competitor David Liederman) comes from Tom Richmond's interesting study, "A Tale of Two Companies," *Inc.,* July 1984, pp. 38–43. Because of the similarity of the products, the David's and Mrs. Fields are an interesting contrast in cultures and leadership styles.

Page 129. The quotes about Lorenzo are taken from "How the Wizard Frank Lorenzo Works His Magic," *Boardroom Reports,* June 1, 1986, p. 4, and "Texas Air Managers Pushed Deregulation Then Put It To Work," *The Wall Street Journal,* March 14, 1986, p. 1.

Page 130. On the difficulties that Conceptuals face once The Venture is established, see Sid Kane, "Your Company . . . or Yourself," *Venture,* June 1985, pp. 98–100. See also Joel Kotkin, "The Smart Team at Compaq Computer," *Inc.,* February, 1986, pp. 48–56, and Sharron Nelton, "Surviving Success in a New Business," *Nation's Business,* December 1984, pp. 20–24.

Page 132. "1-2-3 Creator Mitch Kapor," *Inc.,* January, 1987, p. 32.

CHAPTER EIGHT

Page 135. The epigraph is from Danforth's article, "Handling Change: The Key to Corporate Survival," in Jerome M. Rosow, ed., *Views From The Top* (New York: Facts on File, 1985), p. 89.

Page 135. Brown's definition is given by Harry Levinson, *Executive* (Cambridge, Massachusetts: Harvard University Press, 1981), p. 110.

Page 141. For a descriptive analysis of the different political strategies for dealing with the resistance to change, see John P. Kotter, Leonard A. Schlesinger, and Vijay Sathe, *Organization: Text, Cases, and Readings on the Management of Organizational Design and Change* (Homewood, Illinois: Richard D. Irwin, 1979), pp. 384–92.

Page 150. On the positive value of conflict, see Peter Marris, *Loss and Change* (New York: Pantheon Books, 1974).

Page 152. Sigoloff is quoted in Patricia O'Toole, *Corporate Messiah: The Hiring and Firing of Million-Dollar Managers* (New York: William Morrow, 1984), p. 196.

Pages 156–157. See "High Tech to the Rescue," *Business Week*, June 16, 1986, p. 101.

CHAPTER NINE

Page 161. My thinking on this subject has been much influenced by the work of John Crystal. See the book he wrote with Richard Bolles, *Where Do I Go from Here with My Life?* (New York: Seabury Press, 1974).

Page 161. First epigraph to the chapter from "More Workers Are Saying 'Take This Job Cut and Shove It,' " *Business Week*, December 29, 1986, p. 38. Second epigraph from an interview with a middle manager. (The name has been changed.)

Page 161. Examples taken from a San Francisco *Chronicle* article on unemployed white-collar workers, "A Long Fall from Affluence to Neediness," April 7, 1986, p. 17.

Pages 161–162. Exxon worker quoted in "The End of Corporate Loyalty," *Business Week*, August 4, 1986, p. 48. Example from the Lucky Stores reorganization, San Francisco *Chronicle*, "Reshuffling at Lucky, Gemco," January 20, 1987, p. 22.

Page 165. An interesting analysis of the new roles that are encouraged by rapid change is in Donald Schon, *Beyond the Stable State* (New York: W. W. Norton, 1973), pp. 185–99. See also Beverly Potter, *The Way of the Ronin: A Guide to Career Strategy* (New York: AMACOM, 1984).

Page 170. Eric Berne, *Games People Play* (New York: Grove Press, 1964), pp. 159–62.

Pages 177–178. *Please Understand Me* (Del Mar, California: Prometheus Nemesis Press, 1984) and *Gifts Differing* (Palo Alto, California: Consulting Psychologists Press, 1980).

CHAPTER TEN

Page 183. The quote is from an interview with Bill McGowan, *Inc.,* August 1986, p. 38.

Page 183. *Business Week*, November 5, 1984, pp. 79–86.

Page 185. *In Search of Excellence* (New York: Harper & Row, 1982), p. 156. See the chapter, "Close to Customers," pp. 156–99.

Page 185. The GE example is from Arthur M. Louis, "America's New Economy: How to Manage In It," *Fortune*, June 23, 1986, p. 25.

Page 186. "Changing Skies," *The Wall Street Journal*, March 14, 1986, p. 1. As the example suggests, this kind of action forces an organization into what may be a further transition: from "excellent" behavior to "good enough" behavior. The latter looks like a sellout to many traditional managers, but it may well be essential to moving quickly.

Page 186. "Two Industries Try Speeding Things Up," *Inc.*, May 1986, p. 20.

Page 186. The Drucker quotation is from an interview in *Boardroom Reports,* August 15, 1986, p. 2. Kelly's statement is contained in Ford S. Worthy, "Beatrice's Sell-Off Strategy," *Fortune,* June 23, 1986, p. 44.

Page 187. Examples of computer monitoring are from Bruce G. Posner, "How to Stop Worrying and Love the Next Recession," *Inc.*, April 1986, p. 91.

Pages 188–189. The information on the Army's treatment of the Bradley Fighting Vehicle is given in *Forbes,* July 1, 1985, p. 20. That about FMC and its employee appeared in "Army's Troop Carrier Can't Swim Safely, Critics Say," San Francisco *Chronicle,* September 22, 1986, p. 20.

Pages 189–190. Levinson's quote is from his book, *Executive* (Cambridge: Harvard University Press, 1981), p. 105. The words of Briggs appear in Posner, op. cit., p. 92.

Page 190. *The Change Masters* (New York: Simon & Schuster, 1985), pp. 64–65.

Page 191. For the story of Frost Inc., see Steven P. Galante, "Counting on a Narrow Market Can Cloud Company's Future, *The Wall Street Journal,* January 20, 1986, p. 21, and Curtis Hartman, "Employees as Family," *Inc.,* September 1986, pp. 74–76.

Pages 191–192. The Allen-Bradley assembly line is described in Gene Bylensky, "Breakthrough in Automating the Assembly Line," *Fortune,* May 26, 1986, pp. 64–66. See also John S. DeMott, "In Old Milwaukee: Tomorrow's Factory Today," *Business Week,* June 16, 1986, pp. 66–67.

Page 192. Sharon Rubenstein, "These Temps Don't Just Answer the Phone," *Business Week,* June 2, 1986, p. 74. See also "Professional Temps Fill Top Positions," *Inc.,* February, 1986, p. 98, and "Rent an Executive," San Francisco *Chronicle,* November 26, 1986, p. 21.

Page 193. "The Disposable Employee Is Becoming a Fact of Organizational Life," *Business Week,* December 15, 1986, pp. 52–56.

Page 193. "IBM's Protean Ways," *Datamation,* January 1, 1986, pp. 62–68.

Page 195. Udayan Gupta, "Technology Companies Act to Minimize the Risks of their Ties to IBM," *The Wall Street Journal,* July 10, 1986.

Page 198. Peter Drucker, *Managing in Turbulent Times* (New York: Harper & Row, 1980), p. 45.

Page 200. See Joanne Martin et al., "The Uniqueness Paradox in Organizational Stories," *Research Paper #678,* Graduate School of Business, Stanford University, Palo Alto, California. See also the articles by Alan L. Wilkins, Joanne Martin, and Melanie Powers in Louis R. Pondy et al., eds., *Organizational Symbolism* (Greenwich, Connecticut: JAI Press, 1983), pp. 81–92 and 93–108.

Page 201. An interview with Donald Clifford in *Boardroom Reports,* April 1, 1986, p. 9.

Page 202. Thurow is quoted in "Is the Financial System Shortsighted?" *Business Week,* March 3, 1986, p. 82. The consultant quoted is Lee A. Sage, "How To Keep the Business Strong," *Boardroom Reports* October 15, 1986, p. 6.

Pages 202–203. "Ease the Hardship of Layoffs," *Business Week,* August 4, 1986, p. 84.

INDEX